FIREWALL

FIREWALL

JERRY ROBERT BAIN

ARPress
ILLUMINATING IDEAS
EMPOWERING VOICES

ARPress
45 Dan Road Suite 5
Canton MA 02021
Hotline: 1(888) 821-0229
Fax: 1(508) 545-7580

Ordering Information:
Quantity sales. Special discounts are available on quantity purchases by corporations, associations, and others. For details, contact the publisher at the address above.

Printed in the United States of America.

| ISBN-13: | Softcover | 979-8-89389-546-9 |
| | eBook | 979-8-89389-547-6 |

Library of Congress Control Number: 2021908450

Contents

THEORETICAL CONSTRUCT

The FUNDAMENTAL ASSUMPTION of this SPECULATION is that death WINNOWING by EVOLUTION produced the BRAIN CHEMISTRY that creates our intelligent SELF-CONSCIOUSNESS with a process that SYMBOLIZES life experience as a SIMULATION of causation to make PREDICTIONS for CONSEQUENCES that SATISFY EMOTIONS generated by cellular chemistry programmed with BEHAVIOR INSTINCTS that resulted from selectively KILLING the least COMPETITIVE humans for MILLIONS of GENERATIONS.

This is just like ALL OTHER predator and prey LIFE in the chain of evolution that PASSES on its ESSENCE in a MICROSCOPIC single cell that GROWS into another ADULT for conditional SPECIES IMMORTALITY.

HOWEVER, the RIGIDITY of programmed cellular chemistry also CAUSES us in DIVERGENT circumstances to BE DYSFUNCTIONAL and FAIL to SURVIVE or prosper SO anticipated failure triggers ESCALATION of our instinctive survival programming to STIMULATE conscious CREATIVE INTELLIGENCE to PREDICT and STRATEGIZE proactive preemptory WORK to ADAPT to threat or opportunity.

YET, to PREDICT a SUCCESSFUL strategy, there MUST BE a PROCESS that makes OBJECTIVELY ACCURATE predictions based on a preconceived THEORY of CAUSATION derived from consciously intelligent OBJECTIVE INVESTIGATION using history, simulation, scenarioizing, observation, experimenting, corroboration, theorizing, and TESTING of PATTERNS of PAST EXPERIENCE.

SIMULATING the STORY of human evolution makes a DEFAULT THEORY that gives our conscious intelligence a RELIABLE EXPLANATION of how our INTELLIGENCE and INSTINCTS are DESIGNED to help us survive and prosper.

HOW INTELLIGENT LIFE EVOLVED

THIS evolutionary STRATEGY BEGAN much more than a billion years ago with the INESCAPABLE process of atoms chemically attaching to each other and REPEATEDLY forming molecules that ENTROPY randomly MUTATED until some lasted longer than others and the surviving successions of them lasted longer and longer in a CONTINUOUS PROCESS of lengthening perseveration until SOME lasted long enough to randomly use a perseveration METHOD that PROTECTED them from the chemical environment but also allowed the chemical process that created them to continue SO that the protected molecules could DUPLICATE INSIDE THEIR PROTECTION and thereby DUPLICATE the chemical perseveration and duplication METHOD of the template molecules. This protection became the CELL WALL that contains our GENOME.

In the following BILLIONS of years, the changing earth and the template molecules radically increasing number CHANGED what KIND of protection was NEEDED. However, all the aggregated changes of random mutation left the SURVIVORS protected against an INCOMPREHENSIBLE number and variety of threats which became a PREDICTION of the future environment and a SIMULATION of its CAUSATION which could then evolve PREDICTIONS and PREVENTION of ITS <u>FUTURE</u> DESTRUCTION in at least one CELL that could survive when all the others DIED.

Survivors USED a chemical representation or SIMULATION of the cause and effect rules of physics and chemistry to predict interrupt and REDIRECT the causation chain to create the first PROGRAMMABLE ABSTRACT INTELLIGENCE and this programmed PROCESS was the first behavioral INSTINCT leading to EXTREME intelligence AND that PARTNERSHIP was our <u>BEGINNING</u>.

Yet, it CONTINUES to be the <u>DAILY</u> CHALLENGE of HUMANS to INTEGRATE PREDICTIONS with <u>INSTINCTS</u> to survive/ prosper, find INSTINCTIVE EMOTIONAL FULFILLMENT and create intellectual INSPIRATION for the survival/prosperity of our children.

Instinct and intelligence work TOGETHER the way a computer program <u>TRANSFORMS</u> a box of switches into a predictive algorithm for limited artificial INTELLIGENCE to direct BEHAVIOR like the champion computer chess player BIG BLUE.

THE PLOT THICKENS

THIS prediction and intervention PROCESS for causes and consequences was CODED into the template molecules of the SINGLE FERTILIZED EGG ambulatory life evolved to USE to allow ignorant offspring to SURVIVE and PROSPER in the million generation WAR FOUGHT and WON by predicting and managing consequences using SIMULATION to preemptively prepare for and CHANGE the FUTURE.

It has been a LONG, BLOODY STRUGGLE for you to read this and neither you nor any of your ancestors EARNED or created your SUPERIOR genome. You don't get CREDIT. Entropy MUTATED IT by random chaos to just NATURALLY survive and prosper according to the rules of physics and chemistry.

We owe the LOSERS ALL the GRATITUDE and HONOR for their COURAGE, STRUGGLE, SUFFERING, and SACRIFICE, to GAMBLE for survival and prosperity because THEY CHOSE to ANSWER the CALL to life over millions of years but LOST DESPITE THEIR INNOCENCE so that evolution could bequeath SUCCESS in a SINGLE FERTILIZED EGG with a SLIGHTLY improved genome that grows into an adult to INITIATE preprogrammed EMOTIONS, SURVIVAL BEHAVIORS, and SOCIAL RELATIONSHIPS with cellular chemistry USING DNA, RNA, RNAP, methylation, chromatin, ribosomes, nucleotides, cytokines, chemokine's, nucleic acid, amino acids, acetylcholine, histones, acetates, enzymes, catalytic proteins, etc. WITH COMMUNAL nervous system REGULATION by DIFFERENTIATED NEURON CELL AGGREGATIONS USING selective cell wall and synapse vesicle migration of hormones including vasopressin, dopamine, norepinephrine, serotonin, oxytocin, endorphin, pheromones, etc. and EPIGENETIC chemical and electrical signals to chemically RECORD MEMORY of life experience in a NETWORK of DIFFERENTIATED NEURONS that combine in a neural net like the central processing unit, hard drive, and memory chip, of a computer to create our SELF-AWARE IDENTITY that uses ABSTRACT SYMBOLS in our PROGRAMMABLE CHEMISTRY to CREATE SYMBOLIC INTELLIGENCE that strategizes BEHAVIOR for survival and prosperity.

HOWEVER, DESPITE ENDLESS LABELING and the EXPLOSION of hypothetical EXPLANATIONS for the history, life experience, and chemistry, of our brain, we are STILL BLUNDERING in the DARK to UNDERSTAND predict or CONTROL ourselves each other or aggregated species behavior based on proven REPEATABLE and reliable SCIENCE.

Yet, it is CLEAR that there ARE chemical RULES that HAVE BEEN CONTROLLING us for BILLIONS of years, and we have NO choice except to CONTINUE to ACT on them to LIVE and prosper DESPITE our INADEQUATE explanation, elucidation, or science.

BUT luckily, the INVESTIGATION to DEFINE the RULES of survival and prosperity is ALREADY VERY OLD and our SPECIES has a six thousand-year written <u>HISTORY</u> leading to SEVEN BILLION living individuals following separate evolutionary tracks of adapting, surviving, and prospering, with EACH life being rooted more than a BILLION YEARS ago out of forbearers SURVIVING in diverse environments ultimately using INTELLIGENT SYMBOLIC predictors to MANAGE future events.

These AGGREGATED THEORIES are INSIGHTFUL STORIES that can be PIECED TOGETHER into a SPECULATIVE but CREDIBLE "GESTALT" story of human CREATION, living, and prospering, using NOTHING MORE than HISTORY, CONCRETE EVIDENCE, COMMON SENSE, and CURRENT SCIENCE.

THIS STORY TELLING gives us the "PLOT", "EXPECTATIONS", or "CAUSE and EFFECT", that UNDERLIES all science, and has gotten us VERY FAR down the road to species IMMORTALITY and REAL-WORLD POWER SO, it is LIKELY to RELIABLY TELL our FUTURE and PURPOSE.

EVOLUTIONARY ASSUMPTIONS

It is OBVIOUS that ENVIRONMENTAL forces ALONE CANNOT evolve <u>EXTREME</u> INTELLIGENCE because it is the SPEED and ACCURACY of intelligence to ANTICIPATE <u>COMPLEX</u> CONSEQUENCES that gave us the ADVANTAGE of SYMBOLIC <u>PREDICTIONS</u> <u>OVER</u> biological adaptation that RULES other animals.

The environment is either TOO SLOW or CATASTROPHIC for the INCREMENTAL evolutionary advantage of intelligence and it is NOT SELECTIVE or DISCRIMINATING enough to the cellular chemistry of our central nervous system or EXPLAIN either our technological SUCCESS or why we don't have MORE competition with other species.

Yet, INTRA-species COMPETITION CAN evolve UNLIMITED <u>SUPER </u>intelligence using internal species PREDATION BECAUSE the SMARTEST of us KILLED OFF and robbed every DUMBER person whose survival strategies were LESS EFFECTIVE than OURS over BILLIONS of KILLINGS and GERMINATIONS in our cell line and the MILLIONS of parallel cell lines that WE DESTROYED in GENOCIDE to keep ourselves ALIVE and DOMINANT.

HOW IT STARTED

Before we became human we <u>HAD</u> TO live in PACKS because our claws and jaws were INADEQUATE to survive as solitary hunters SO the INTERNAL species COMPETITION focused on HIERARCHICAL <u>SOCIAL</u> INSTINCTS instead of <u>PHYSICAL</u> LETHALITY and evolution AMPLIFIED this <u>MENTAL</u> COMPETITION with behavior instincts of EGO, greed, envy, ANGER, revenge, hate, sadism, distrust, and INTENSIFIED HIERARCHICAL social AMBITION.

THIS PRODUCED the <u>FIRST</u> EVOLUTIONARY ENHANCEMENT of INTELLIGENCE because those that were ALIVE after the inevitable KILLING were the MOST EFFECTIVELY lethal STRATEGIZERS but CHEMICALLY, INSTINCTIVELY, and EMOTIONALLY, so ALIENATED from EACH OTHER that they could even VICTIMIZE their own FAMILY to become the "GRIM REAPERS" of evolution that MURDERED, INTIMIDATED, and COERCED, <u>ANYONE</u> less lethally cunning than themselves WHENEVER it served their own personal ADVANTAGE, EGO, and INSTINCTIVE EMOTIONS. Otherwise, they manipulated the PROTECTION and POWER of the PACK to their own advantage. BETRAYAL was their cutting edge.

THESE WERE the FIRST PSYCHOPATHS and over the next million years they made us very SMART by KILLING EVERYONE they could to loot, or enslave, as well as ALL the DUMBER family and peers in their own clan. In modern terms they were very successful CRIMINALS and VICTIMIZERS who ran GANGS that used violence and terror to enslave us. They became our OVERLORDS and even claimed nobility or GODHOOD to CONFOUND our intelligence.

PREDATORY PRESSURE had not only MADE us OUTSMART each other to SURVIVE and PROSPER but after we developed LANGUAGE we ORGANIZED SUPERIOR clans, tribes, and armies, to ENSLAVE other groups of humans using the DIVERSITY of our NUMBERS to RECRUIT gifted warriors, CREATIVE technical COMBAT advantages, specialized teamwork, STRATEGIC analysis for planning, and MASSIVE social aggregation of our members to organize BIGGER more EFFECTIVE social implementation for WAR and the recruiting of food.

This AGGREGATION and ORGANIZATION for WAR succeeded because we gave conquered people a CHOICE of DYING or WORKING under the arbitrary control of a slave master. HOWEVER, only the most INSTINCTIVELY HIERARCHICAL of them were CAPABLE of being aware of and MOTIVATED by the MENTAL INTENT of another person. SO those that were TOO impulsive, aggressive, self-centered, antisocial, psychopathic, egotistical, or could not consistently IDENTIFY and TEACH THEMSELVES to perform complex tasks in social relationships or TEAMS of other people to satisfy the needs and WISHES of a MASTER WERE WORKED TO DEATH or tortured as examples.

The GRIM REAPER of INTELLIGENCE and submission to SLAVERY was kept VERY busy by war, oppression of slaves, and hierarchical subordination, disciplining, and winnowing of their own organization for hundreds of thousands of years.

This WINNOWING left SURVIVORS who had the ability to ANTICIPATE and maintain intuitive peer relationships and EFFECTIVE TEAMWORK to PLEASE the overlord and slave master but also have MENTAL and PHYSICAL abilities beyond the OVERLORD which he CO-OPTED to claim the GENIUS as a MESSIAH, for himself and CONFOUND our intelligence with AWED SELF DOUBT.

However, this only left alive those strongly motivated by FEAR who still had enough OBJECTIVITY to think creatively and EFFECTIVELY about PROBLEMS in fulfilling the IMAGINATION of the overlord. Those left after the winnowing had the LEARNING ABILITY to TEACH THEMSELVES to think and BELIEVE like their VICTIMIZERS, to make GOOD SOLDIERS, to capture more slaves, govern by TERROR, or support the high lifestyle of the WARLORD, as well as their own.

The Roman Empire PERFECTED this but they are JUST the ones that left records and it must have gone on for hundreds of thousands of years among ALL humans or they were EXTERMINATED by WARRIOR SOCIETIES.

This death winnowing EVOLVED cellular chemistry for offspring to have diverse instinctive social behaviors driven by EMOTIONS that DICTATE social organization which we loosely call SOCIAL INSTINCT or EMPATHY, and it preferentially developed in women because they needed it as MOTHERS to care for their children till they could become self-sufficient. The children became OBSESSIVE-COMPULSIVE about HELPING.

EMPATHY was so valuable that survival favored it as EGO IDENTITY FUSION that ENMESHED the personality of entire families so they all had the same instinctive emotion triggers, perceived and interpreted their life experience in the same way, had the same values, and pursued common goals.

There are many OTHER components of this social instinct like affection, social anxiety, envy, shame, inspiration, humor, resentment, ambition, hate, ego, infatuation, etc., that evolved as social organization got bigger and more complex and COMPETED with OTHER hierarchical cultures for ORGANIZATIONAL DOMINANCE through strategic war and trade for life enhancing goods.

Most of the men DIED, in the winnowing by warlords because they were too instinctively DOMINANT as WARRIORS to accept control and because of limited ability to adapt their social RELATIONSHIPS, but the children of the warlord or slave master and the female slaves were more docile and made BETTER SLAVES more easily TRAUMATIZED into REACTION FORMATION that made them BELIEVE whatever BEHAVIOR EXPECTATIONS, RATIONALIZATIONS, and SOCIAL THEORY, they were told in order to survive AT ANY COST and a SLAVE SOCIETY was BRED motivated, and organized by WILLING EMPATHIC SUBMISSION to AUTHORITY or they were worked to death, crucified as examples of rebellion, killed as TERROR acts, or used for military training.

ORGANIZED WARFARE put our cellular chemistry under INTENSELY PROFOUND SELECTION for BOTH individual and socially AGGREGATED intelligence linked by COMPLEX SOCIAL INSTINCTS that CREATED DISTRIBUTED INTELLIGENCE linking MULTIPLE INTELLIGENT INDIVIDUALS, organized as ARMIES, or work teams, that were in constant military conflict preparation for WAR, massive building, domestic or economic activities, and LETHAL INTERNAL SELECTIVE PRESSURE for a better personal lifestyle.

This was LIKE the movie *Highlander* where the ONLY RULE DICTATED "THERE CAN BE ONLY ONE" and psychopaths ruthlessly created population BOTTLENECKS that almost exterminated us more than once when drought, overpopulation, or disease, ALSO HIT.

WHY IT WAS INEVITABLE

HOWEVER, in the half a million years <u>BEFORE</u> that our RUTHLESS PREDATION on each other had ALREADY forced EVOLUTION to make a <u>SECOND</u> ENHANCEMENT of intelligence, that temporarily avoided EXTINCTION by CONTINUOUS SEXUAL LUST to MAKE more BABIES.

EVOLUTION MUTATED the survival ADVANTAGE of SEXUALLY released OXYTOCIN and other hormones, like vasopressin, endorphin, dopamine, and norepinephrine to chemically MAKE the FATHER and MOTHER of the family of origin ADDICTED to creating PAIR BONDING, COMMON FAMILY GOALS, and HIERARCHICALLY organized teamwork that made the family ACT as a single unit using specialized jobs to HUNT and FEED by FIGHTING DOMINANCE that selected for INTELLIGENT ORGANIZED HUNTING, SUBMISSION to HIERARCHY, and WARFARE.

INSTINCTIVE SEXUAL ADDICTION, IDENTITY FUSION, and the EMPATHIC ability to predict the instinctive social personality of men gave WOMEN the POWER to predict which MEN would EMPATHICALLY FUSE their instinctive self-aware IDENTITY with them SO that their children had a FATHER who would PROTECT and PROVIDE for their FAMILY of ORIGIN with INTELLIGENT HUNTING and RUTHLESS PREDATORY FURY against enemies. FAMILY was EVERYTHING.

SO, the <u>FIFTH</u> EVOLUTIONARY enhancement of INTELLIGENCE was an INSTINCTIVE PASSION for LOVE ABLE to MOVE mountains.

Larger families and LENGTHENED adolescence allowed NON-LETHAL competition of children as PLAY to better prepare them to SURVIVE/PROSPER. So LONGER CHILDHOOD was a <u>THIRD</u> evolutionary ENHANCEMENT of INTELLIGENCE.

Which gave time and survival advantage to parents who EMOTIONALLY IDENTIFIED with their children to FUSE their instinctive EGO with them as they had already done with each other and MENTALLY SIMULATE their children's THOUGHTS, FEELINGS, probable BEHAVIOR, and NEEDS, to better TEACH THEM SURVIVAL SKILLS using MIRROR NEURONS that BOOSTED the mental simulation to emotionally AMPLIFY empathy, and made the children EMPATHICALLY <u>WANT</u> to IMITATE their PARENTS. So, IDENTITY-FUSION-EMPATHY had become the <u>FOURTH</u> evolutionary enhancement of INTELLIGENCE.

RELIGION

Yet SEXUAL INFATUATION, IDENTITY FUSION, EMPATHY, and ALL the other social INSTINCTS that differentiate behavior did far more than drive family and community organization because its EMOTIONS DICTATE an INSTINCTIVE BEHAVIOR STRATEGY that comes from a hidden and rationally unknowable place OUTSIDE our senses, conscious common sense, intelligence, understanding, predictability, or rational purpose, but DEMANDS very specific ORCHESTRATED SOCIAL BEHAVIORS WITHOUT a way to intelligently PREDICT WHAT THEY ARE.

However, to PREDICT we must CREATE a conscious THEORY of causation for our creative intelligence to PREDICT effective STRATEGIC planning and behaviors.

ALL INSTINCTIVE EMOTIONS follow this PATTERN of consciously unknown assumptions and PURPOSE driving behavior with NO consciously intelligent THEORETICAL WAY to strategize and PLAN behaviors that <u>MUST</u> RESOLVE chemically driven emotions to survive and prosper.

In fact, there is NO WAY to CONSCIOUSLY KNOW the difference between instinct and consciously intelligent choice because INTELLIGENCE is DESIGNED to JUSTIFY, STRATEGIZE, ACT OUT, and RESOLVE INSTINCTIVE EMOTION as a single

CONTINUOUS process. Intelligence is a SLAVE to instinct but can only ACHIEVE what serves EVOLUTION FIRST

Self-reflection is NOT an inherent part of the instinct/intelligence partnership and MUST be imposed by fully conscious choice DESPITE opposition by our own instinctive emotions which are designed to FORCE behavior COMPLIANCE with our instinctive cellular chemistry.

The THEORIES that must be IMPROVISED for instinctive COMMUNAL living inevitably become personal and community RELIGIONS because there is NO rational or logical causation PROCESS or theory for intelligence to make and VERIFY predictive simulations for group management of EMOTIONS or VALUES.

Yet, since we survive by predicting causation we DO THEORIZE and the most obvious and easiest THEORY to inevitably evolve is that the IMPULSIVE EMOTIONS that OBVIOUSLY urge our BEHAVIOR come from a DIFFERENT PERSON like in our FAMILY or CLAN HIERARCHY but able to INJECT the IMPERATIVE to ACT directly into our mind and any CONTRADICTIONS are the CONFLICT of two or more of these SUPERNATURAL beings.

Therefore, the external AUTHORITY and CONTROL that urges us to obey MUST have an intent, purpose, or THEORY, we COULD use to ANTICIPATE and prepare to PLEASE them if we knew it and depend on their GRATITUDE to give us a better future, just the way WE already do in our own organized family and community HIERARCHY, AS SLAVES.

The simplest common sense to theorize this ignorance is that the SUPERNATURAL PERSONALITY would be like us or our SLAVE-MASTER but with VASTLY SUPERIOR INTELLIGENCE and POWER BEYOND our UNDERSTANDING.

In WAR, we are weak INDIVIDUALLY and strong in groups so another GROUP POWER greater than ourselves that controls EVERYONE might help us if we enslave ourselves to them the way we have already done for many generations to the WARLORD. We must WORSHIP, SERVE, and BELIEVE.

It also STRONGLY helps manage DISABLING FEAR if RESPONSIBILITY is NOT on US to resolve it.

IDENTITY FUSION instinctively makes it seem obvious that these SUPERNATURAL BEINGS MUST HAVE the SAME AUTHORITY over ALL OTHER PEOPLE and expects ALL humans to comply with the same THEORY of BEHAVIOR we BELIEVE they or HE expects us to follow. Certainly, SLAVES must OBEY or SUFFER.

That inevitably creates multiple improvable THEORIES to EXPLAIN ancient inherently DIVERSE, chemical behavior instincts to resolve or control the emotions generated by life experience, SO it is INEVITABLE that there would be an ENDLESS NUMBER of MUTATING, EVOLVING, RELIGIONS, IMPORTANT enough to INSTINCTIVELY intellectually define cultural values, LIVE, and even KILL for, but are spawned by the DIVERSITY of cellular chemistry that responds DIFFERENTLY to DIVERSE CIRCUMSTANCE. Religion MUTATES with evolution and diverse aggregated BELIEF SYSTEMS are VERY vulnerable to CORRUPTION by psychopaths.

However, they are not ALWAYS called or recognized as RELIGIONS and may be labeled FAMILY, FRIENDS, ACHIEVEMENT, PRIDE, LOYALTY, CULTURE, PATRIOTISM, MILITARY, career, government, ambition, conquest, business, survival, politics, self-defense, philosophy, values, social activism, mysticism, paranormal, ART, hobbies, sports, etc., but ALL EXPRESS INSTINCTIVE EMOTION as complex behavior that may use MORE THAN ONE expression to SATISFY, FULFILL, or RESOLVE, enough instinctive INTERPRETATION of PLEASURE to trigger and DRIVE the ancient chemistry of PASSION to CREATE that DRIVES ALL the objectively disciplined behaviors needed for survival and prosperity.

People that don't COMPLY to our own religion INSTINCTIVELY seem ALIEN, or EVIL SO they are SUSPICIOUS and MIGHT BE ENEMIES and therefore WOULD DESERVE to be victimized as our justified prey. They might NOT be HUMAN but VERY dangerous in SURPRISING WAYS.

RELIGION ATTRACTS criminals, psychopaths, con artists, mentally disturbed, poor, powerless, and abused people the way light attracts moths. THAT is where the AUTHORITY of the COMMUNITY IS and BLIND, unconditional BELIEVING offers an opportunity for ANYONE to get help and POWER by submitting to CONTROL by other people to BELIEVE anything they say and DO what they want.

This is a recipe for IRRATIONAL, IRRESOLVABLE, social CONFLICT.

YET, the WISDOM of ancient INSTINCT took ETERNITY to CREATE survival and PROSPERITY for our species in ways we can only guess at but is so DEEP in ancient cellular chemistry and instinctive protection/prosperity that we don't DARE diddle with it for fear of UNRAVELING our cellular chemistry with all its social instincts like EMPATHY, COMPASSION, IDENTITY FUSION, INFATUATION, JOY, pride, shame, fear, inspiration, envy, anger, lust, etc., the way a small bump TUMBLES a house of cards and DESTROYS our specie's BALANCE between instinct and objective intelligence.

Therefore, our own cellular chemistry FORCES us to CONSCIOUSLY CHOOSE whether to CONTINUE PREYING on and victimizing each other for the sake of selfish advantage/revenge OR defend each other from entropy and psychopaths by INTEGRATING, FUSING, and CREATING SELF-AWARENESS of SPECIES LEVEL

INTELLIGENCE with empathy and compassion for our suffering and dying. This is the way our individual neurons WAKE UP in the morning to become <u>US</u> or the way our SOUL wakes up and goes to WORK with the rest of our society.

By choosing to remain predators we LIMIT the objective fluid intelligence at the species level and continue to EMBRACE the PSYCHOPATHIC hate, SADISM, revenge, persecution, deception, exploitation, depression, fear, grief, suffering, etc., that CREATED us and <u>WILL</u> go <u>ON</u> creating the SUPREME WARRIOR of DEATH to everything "NOT SELF".

OR we could GIVE UP those predatory INSTINCTS with personal and public RELIGIOUS THEORY that organizes their DECONDITIONING using CLASSICAL CONDITIONING, MEDITATION, DAYDREAMING, and PRAYER.

HOWEVER, DEFACTO our species has ALREADY MADE this choice when EMPATHY and COMPASSION evolved to bind us together in wise and LOVING ways as a nurturing distributed CREATIVELY INTELLIGENT social organism.

INSTINCT INEVITABLY RESULTED in creative ABSTRACTIONS like angels and demons that ancient RELIGIONS evolved to SYMBOLIZE, EXPRESS, and MANAGE, behavioral instinct but MUST now BE INTELLIGENTLY and OBJECTIVELY DECONSTRUCTED to allow our CREATIVE INTELLIGENCE to build our INDIVIDUAL and SPECIES FIREWALL containing religious METAPHOR that can be USED to teach ethics, morality, WISE behavior, social concepts and dynamics, religious theory, and consensus building, for maturing children to become competent in the planning of community goals, priorities, and work organization.

SO, the myth of SUPERNATURAL BEINGS can STILL be used to INVEST a modern RELIGIOUS RITUAL needed for classical conditioning of EMOTION in PUBLIC and personal religious theory that predicates commitment and compliance to an aggregated community BELIEF SYSTEM and its support, goals, organization, obligations, methods, and, sacrifice.

However, the BLIND FAITH of childhood MUST MATURE and OPEN its MIND to the REALITY of causation. SO, since we are all instinctively UNIQUE, each of us should CONSCIOUSLY and INTELLIGENTLY CREATE OUR OWN unique, individual RELIGIOUS BELIEFS in the PRIVACY of our personal FIREWALL.

Most EMOTIONS like empathy, identity fusion, compassion, sexual infatuation, shame, envy, resentment, pride, etc., EVOLVED to socially LINK and BOND us ALL together CHEMICALLY in a SPECIES level IDENTITY. YET, community religion is only an aggregated DERIVATIVE of cellular chemistry, and not RIGID, like we are CHEMICALLY.

Therefore, a PUBLIC RELIGION can be FREE of the dead hand of our gnomically driven emotions to DEMOCRATICALLY DEFINE our community THEOLOGY out of the symbols of our lifestyle to strategize a FIREWALL for the empowerment of COMMUNITY and SPECIES values, priorities, purpose, methods, goals, consensus, organization, etc. This is our GOVERNMENT!

Evolution is NOT a traditional religion, despite being a belief system, because it is based on cellular chemistry, instincts, science, and current lifestyle, instead of BLIND FAITH belief in a two thousand-year-old PARABLE using examples of a murderous OVERLORD government in a slave driven society to CURRENTLY teach empathy and compassion to 7 billion people able to quickly access EACH OTHER and most written knowledge, computer BROWSED, for facts, scientific investigation, and interpretation.

Therefore, an aggregated <u>PUBLIC</u> religion should be defined by a democratic consensus DERIVED from creatively intelligent assessment of scientifically verified INSTINCTS. SO, there can be a community religious FIREWALL in GOVERNMENT.

The value of a PUBLIC RELIGION is to provide a theoretical context for distributed community intelligence to guide, analyze, evaluate, prioritize, select, organize, and condition, COMMON PURPOSE, goals, processes, methods, plans, commitments, resources, and action, SO it should be EVOKED and RITUALIZED in public gatherings when important community decisions are to be made as the SYMBOLIC BASIS of the CALL to ORGANIZED COMMUNITY action, participation, contribution, compliance, sacrifice, and commitment.

PUBLIC religion MUST <u>NEVER</u> apply to <u>ANY</u> specific individual and PERSONAL religion MUST <u>ONLY</u> apply to <u>THAT</u> individual and THAT rule should be formalized and enforced in the public FIREWALL of the GOVERNMENT CONSTITUTION TO prevent PERSECUTION of individuals for their FREE choice of personal religion or THEIR attempts to FORCE their personal theological/ instinctive beliefs on other people including their children.

SEXUAL DIFFERENTIATION

At some very early point SEXUAL IDENTITY became DIFFERENTIATED with larger MALES being DESIGNED to KILL by being INSTINCTIVELY MORE COMBATIVE, FEARLESS, COMPETITIVE, IMPULSIVE, HYPERACTIVE, DOMINEERING, arrogant, self-centered, cunning, ruthless, deceptive, jealous, vengeful, territorial, object oriented, possessive, obsessive, compulsive, narrowly focused, thrill seeking, risk seeking, ATHLETIC, higher metabolism, etc. that FACILITATED them being a KILLING MACHINE and INEVITABLY GETTING KILLED to WINNOW each other for the SMARTEST.

FEMALES became DESIGNED to SURVIVE and to CARE for their children by having SUPERIOR SOCIAL, SYMBOLIC, and EMOTIONAL INTELLIGENCE, with INSTINCTIVE PROGRAMMING for SELF-PROTECTION by ANXIETY, EMPATHY, IDENTITY FUSION, shame, social context, better incidental memory, superior fine motor coordination, high pain tolerance, etc.

MEN BECAME CANNON FODDER in the RAMPAGING WAR of EVOLUTION for POWER over CHALLENGE to survival/prosperity and WOMEN BECAME the PRIZE they FOUGHT and DIED to POSSES FUSE their IDENTITY with, PROVIDE for, and PROTECT.

This meant that WOMEN were subject to the power of psychopathic men and therefore got ABUSED and VICTIMIZED by intimidation, privation, exploitation, deception, manipulation, coercion, fear, and trauma, that triggered REACTION FORMATION to confound their creative intelligence and make them PERMANENT willing SLAVES smarter than their masters.

However, women MIGHT COVERTLY select the WINNER of the competition between men using their SUPERIOR MIND READING EMPATHY, social connections, and INTELLIGENCE. This CUTTING EDGE made them and their children EVEN SMARTER.

CONTINUOUS SEXUAL INFATUATION, LENGTHENED child nurturing, empathic MIRROR NEURONS, identity FUSION, and PARENTS who could STAND UPRIGHT to wield weapons and CARRY FOOD home, ALLOWED the RUTHLESS PREDATION of men to CONTINUE winnowing each other for intelligence even while hierarchical families, submissive to a PATRIARCH, but CENTERED around the family lifestyle of WOMEN, NURTURED replacements to REPLENISH our species.

LANGUAGE

Early in our evolution the SOCIAL and life experience conditions caused us to LEARN to ASSOCIATE SPOKEN SOUNDS with LIFE EXPERIENCES and USE them to SYMBOLIZE, GENERALIZE, DIFFERENTIATE, DISCRIMINATE, ASSOCIATE, and ORGANIZE THINKING.

Speech let us SHARE observations and interpretations to GET AHEAD OF the SLOWNESS of the KILLING and DYING of EVOLUTION as well as ALL other concrete causation to make PREDICTIONS then TELL them to PEERS for PARALLEL communal problem solving, SELECTION, and IMPLEMENTATION, in MASSIVE hierarchal social ORGANIZATION for war and food.

Language also created the conditions for a PUBLIC RELIGION that could build a shared CONSENSUS on community values, purpose, GOALS, priorities, and ORGANIZE community work, hunting, food gathering/preparation, and WAR.

THE use of LANGUAGE operated as though we could READ EACH OTHER'S MINDS to RADICALLY INCREASE SPECIES INTELLIGENCE by LINKING individuals into a DISTRIBUTED INTELLIGENT PROCESS or social WEB of symbolic analysis and prediction of consequences for COMMUNAL WORK and WAR.

Women were SUPERIOR to men with language and religion because they were <u>MORE</u> socially motivated, integrated, and NETWORKED, by empathy, identity fusion, envy, shame, anxiety, INTELLIGENCE, and the social context of church, than men who used language and religion to COMPETE, CONTROL, SEEK, and USE POWER.

SYMBOLIC THINKING

LANGUAGE WAS the <u>SIXTH ENHANCEMENT</u> of INTELLIGENCE but it was BASED on CYBER SYMBOLISM that opened the door to a WHOLE NEW UNIVERSE of evolutionary processes able to CREATE UNLIMITED intelligence because MENTAL SYMBOLS are free to EVOLVE far faster than the killing and dying that drives evolution of cellular chemistry to RADICALLY IMPROVE our behavioral STRATEGIES, RELIGIOUS SYMBOLISM, and METHODS, at the SPEED of SOUND.

PARALLEL PROCESSING by MULTIPLE INDIVIDUALS CREATES MULTIPLE PREDICTIONS so the most accurate THEORY can be RECRUITED by our aggregated social organization then TRANSFERRED into ENORMOUS culturally organized hierarchical WORK, SOCIAL, RELIGIOUS, and WAR groups, as one DISTRIBUTED MIND to form a single organism, and ARMY out of an entire community, tribe, culture, religion, or civilization.

THIS WAS probably DONE with STORY TELLING and RELIGIOUS INTERPRETATION, probably mainly by women CAREFULLY REHEARSING creative intelligence with their men because their better gnomically programmed social instincts, experience, and intelligence, better programmed them to protect and nurture their children, and EVERYONE in their FAMILY.

Men probably co-opted, manipulated, DOMINATED, and CONTROLLED this process to GET and KEEP POWER using psychopathic ruthlessness over OTHER PEOPLE'S abilities the way WARLORDS and OVERLORDS recruited slave organizations to FULFILL their imagination.

TOOL USE

THIS SYMBOLIC language PROCESSING greatly CATALYZED and ACCELERATED transmission of TOOL USE and TECHNOLOGY EXPLODED across all cultural divides BECAUSE IDEAS COMMUNICATE like a VIRUS to PUT a WEAPON in the HANDS of the GRIM REAPERS of WAR and a cutting tool for skinning, butchering, and reaping, by food gatherers and workers just by WATCHING and TALKING with peers.

TOOL USE WAS a <u>SEVENTH</u> ENHANCEMENT of the EVOLUTION of INTELLIGENCE by INTENSIFYING the WINNOWING by predatory DEATH and improving the recruiting of food.

WRITING

After a half million years of HIERARCHICAL TRIBES hunting, gathering food, WAGING war, and two hundred thousand using LANGUAGE, we began generational passing of property, tradition, culture, history, and organizational RULES that was complex enough to NEED to CREATE a WRITING SYSTEM for our SYMBOLIC LANGUAGE perhaps ten thousand years ago to BRIDGE the gap in KNOWLEDGE created by FREQUENT DEATH, war, social conflict, revolution, coup-de-tat, starvation, disease, religious indoctrination, reorganization, population dislocation, ignorance, catastrophe, or WAR, probably by men to strengthen their POWER STRUCTURE so it could be passed to their sons, families, and allies.

WRITING CREATES an IMMORTAL SUPERNATURAL TEACHER from OUTSIDE our life experience, family, community, tribe, culture, and civilization, like a new kind of cellular chemistry to CREATE an EIGHTH ENHANCEMENT of INTELLIGENCE to RELIABLY TEACH SUCCEEDING GENERATIONS or ALIENATED, disenfranchised, community members relevant, useful information and its interpretation, evaluation, and analysis, FREE from the PREDATION of WARLORDS using TERROR, DEATH, ENSLAVEMENT, COERCION, intimidation, deception, manipulation, indoctrination, propaganda, poverty, starvation, corruption, and ignorance.

COMPUTERS HAVE now MADE a <u>NINTH</u> CYBER ENHANCEMENT of intelligence LINKED through the INTERNET that MAKES ALL socially aggregated, real time, COMPREHENSIVE KNOWLEDGE and ANALYSIS an INTEGRAL PART of our INDIVIDUAL and AGGREGATED SPECIE'S KNOWLEDGE to create a species level distributed creative intelligence at the speed of electricity linking us together.

This is like comprehensive INHERITED WISDOM.

However, this technology can be perverted by BIG MONEY using computerized demographics to split our votes and tell us what we want to hear AND MORE OF IT while they QUIETLY hold workshops and CAUCUS in luxury resorts with VERY SMART CONSULTANTS, CEO'S, CFO'S, governors, politicians, lawyers, etc. manipulating money.

SUPERNATURAL EVOLUTION

We now have COMPUTER PROGRAMS that create intelligent processes as BROWSERS and SEARCH ENGINES, networked to most written KNOWLEDGE that can CORRELATE, analyze, hypothesize, simulate, and corroborate, our functional intelligence with "survival of the fittest" computer EVOLUTION of PROGRAMS for creative cyber processes that enhance ECONOMIC/FINANCIAL ANALYSIS, TRADE for LIFE ENHANCING GOODS, social analysis and organization, goal strategizing, resource management, government administration, and scientific knowledge.

WE have now BECOME a COMPUTER ENHANCED, EMPATHICALLY LINKED CYBERNETIC LIFE FORM at the BRINK of CREATING an ELEVENTH ENHANCEMENT of INTELLIGENCE by directly linking to neuron cell chemistry with DRUGS, ELECTRICAL STIMULATION, and CHANGING our own GENOME to MANIPULATE instinctive emotions and electrical brain functions to EXTERNALLY PROGRAM our mental experience.

It is NOW CLEAR that someday our ENTIRE SPECIES could be a SINGLE CREATIVELY INTELLIGENT ENTITY of its own or several the SAME WAY INDIVIDUAL brain NEURONS aggregate, differentiate, and integrate, USING axons and synapses to BECOME specialized brain functions that are INTEGRATED to define YOU.

CYBERSPACE

THIS CYBERSPACE we create in the neuron web of our brain, HOUSES, PROTECTS, and EMPOWERS our symbolized EMOTIONS, instincts, religion, intuitions, life experience, interpretations, values, meaning, ideas, concepts, INTELLIGENCE, and purpose, AS WELL AS our AGGREGATED social instincts, and their religion.

This is our SOUL, and it lives as long as our species does because it is not PHYSICAL and has no LIMITATIONS just the way a COMPUTER PROGRAM is TOTALLY DETACHED from the computer hardware that runs it and LIKEWISE our soul is BEYOND the POWER, CONTROL, and LIMITS, of the CAUSATION of this UNIVERSE and ALL its LAWS of physics, chemistry, entropy, mutation, other people, and even the aggregated enhanced intelligence of our community because WE ARE A holographic SIMULATION projected by the neuron web of our brain.

CYBERSPACE GIVES us the SUPERNATURAL FREEDOM and power to be SELF-AWARE in ANY purely imaginary symbolic construct BELIEF SYSTEM or RELIGION and even CHANGE REALITY or the past with reinterpretation and TESTING NOW for TRUTH lost to time, entropy, and mutation.

This happens EVERY TIME we read a fictional story for fun. Or watch TV.

WIKIPEDIA, SEARCH ENGINES, and fictional literature ARE an ANALOGY of CYBERSPACE where EVERYONE has INPUT to RECORD or DELETE and the information is "crowd" and computer assisted to EVOLVE scenarios and simulations into CORRELATION and INTEGRATION that systematically hypothesize and strategize multiple simulations to test THEORIES on possible futures. We designed it to work like us.

15

BELIEVING

This is BELIEVING and it RUNS the UNIVERSE because IT is the HUMAN MIND that CONSTRUCTS our INTERPRETATION of our LIFE SO IT MUST BE DONE in the PRIVATE CYBERSPACE of our BRAIN where it is free of the dead hand of our social obligations as well as the PHYSICS and CHEMISTRY of this UNIVERSE.

IT is MORE than EGOTISM when our CHOICES define REALITY because the human MIND is an INDUCTIVE, DEDUCTIVE, COMPARING, CONTRASTING, DIFFERENCE PREDICTING, and EXPECTING MACHINE that is constantly scenarioizing and simulating MANY CONTINGENCY CAUSE-EFFECT TIME LINES SO that we can CHOOSE ONE to move INTO.

IT IS our BELIEF in our CYBERSPACE CREATIONS that RELEASES the central nervous system chemicals that DICTATE the homeostatic chemical program of INFATUATION, evolved to MAKE BABIES, but EXPANDED by evolution to LOCK on to IDEAS as THOUGH they are CHILDREN of the future.

Our conscious CHOICE of behavior is ALWAYS in SERVICE to a BELIEF in a future NOT YET TRUE and THREATENED by mistakes, faulty predictions, ignorance, emotions, self-deception, delusions, mutation, and entropy, SO we MUST become OBSESSED and COMPULSIVE about NURTURING and PROTECTING our DREAMS as though they are CHILDREN.

THE UNPROVEN ASSUMPTIONS of INSTINCT and their expression as RELIGION are CRITICAL to the appropriate release of VITAL NEUROCHEMICALS needed to resolve STRESS, STRUGGLE, and DYSPHORIA, because disappointment, fatigue, exhaustion, and FAILURE are COMMON and the THREAT of it constantly DRIVES us to CONCENTRATE our whole mind on WORK for success in a future we CANNOT be SURE of while we worry about FAILURE and the DEPRESSIVE ANXIETY of cognitive dissonance that FOLLOWS.

Our CURRENT happiness depends on the expectation of JOY and FULFILLMENT to come SO it is the STRENGTH of our BELIEVING that is CRITICAL to the chemical release of hormones that POWERS the CHEMISTRY of our brain, body, work, and SYMBOLIC INTELLIGENCE.

This MEANS that the PLACEBO EFFECT, BELIEVING, and RELIGION, are MORE POWERFUL than TRUTH, in giving us fulfillment and satisfaction. HOWEVER, IN THIS UNIVERSE we must SACRIFICE and ENDURE PAIN to find and secure OBJECTIVE TRUTH and few achieve it because it has a troublesome sibling of SELF-DECEPTION that gets all the resources.

EVERY SCIENTIST DOES THIS when they CONCEIVE an experiment to test and CORROBORATE a theory, or engineers IMPLEMENT a theory with the investment of time, effort, and resources, to BUILD NEW TECHNOLOGY, or ARCHITECTS design empowered living spaces to FACILITATE SURVIVAL, PROSPERITY, inspiration, and EVOLUTION, through the VISIONARY FUNCTIONAL symbolism of LIVING spaces.

COMPUTER GAMES and interactive <u>SIMULATIONS</u> are ALREADY TRAINING US to enter and run artificially created CYBER REALITIES that can SIMULATE limited SCENARIOS to EVOLVE social CONCEPTS, and NO human gets abused, exploited, coerced, terrorized, victimized, sacrificed, or dies.

THESE SIMULATIONS will INEVITABLY BECOME smarter than us just by AGGREGATION because test SIMULATION of alternate SCENARIOS lets us get ahead of the future and super computers lets us MASSIVELY test simulations of scenarios simultaneously. Evolution did the same thing with millions of years.

This is the essence of EVOLUTIONARY PROBLEM SOLVING even though it is FINANCED by internet advertising; the TECHNOLOGY of CREATIVE INTELLIGENCE will run everything BUT our ancient GENOME and its network of INSTINCTIVE EMOTIONS that give us a PASSION to CREATE and a HOME for our SOUL in CYBERSPACE.

YET, We MUST have an INSTINCTIVE IMPULSE to TARGET CONSEQUENCES important to survival and prosperity to give us the DIRECTION to start WINNOWING rational mutations of problem solving or goal setting with SCIENCE to simulate for survival and prosperity then TEST for the best by EXPERIMENT.

Our objective INTELLECT WAITS without emotion for our INSTINCT and RELIGION to assign INSTINCTIVE VALUE, MEANING, PURPOSE, INTENTION, and PRIORITY, to our preparation for the future. THEN, CREATIVE INTELLIGENCE <u>GOES TO WORK.</u>

16

INFATUATION

However, the germination for the PASSION of PURPOSE is to FALL in love and make it our mistress. TRUTH should be worshiped as the will of GOD and our WORK is to use it to serve me/us. We must symbolize our LUST in terms of survival and prosperity for us and our species.

This is OVERARCHING LOVE that DRIVES conscious intelligence with an INSTINCTIVE IMPERATIVE that makes us OBSESSIVE-COMPULSIVE and OBLIVIOUS of sacrifice, to nurture the future of our CHILDREN.

INFATUATION is the "SAVING GRACE" that OVERRIDES and COMPENSATES us for ALL the anxiety, self-doubt, ambivalence, self-discipline, work, struggle, sacrifice, suffering, grief, trauma, and atrocities we GO THROUGH EVERY DAY to SURVIVE and PROSPER.

LOVE BACKS US UP when EVERYTHING ELSE FAILS and we WANT to GIVE UP and DIE or LASH OUT and DESTROY everything in an EXPLOSION of HATE or everything else MAKES us SELL OUT our creative intelligence and social conscience for CORRUPT concepts and BLOCKS TRAUMA from MAKING us SLAVES to psychopaths.

SEXUAL PASSION was EXPANDED by our creative intelligence and empathy to INSPIRE the OBSESSIONS, ideas, beliefs, concepts, and compulsions we NEED to provide for a family so POWERFULLY that we will DO ANYTHING NECESSARY to LIVE by them.

MAGNIFICENT OBSESSIONS are our ULTIMATE FULFILLMENT because the POWER of symbolic BELIEVING unites INSTINCT and INTELLECT to RELEASE the ECSTASY and JOY of cellular chemistry that LIGHTS UP our brain circuits to TURN a SYMBOLIZED "DREAM", INSPIRATION, or EPIPHANY into a pragmatic PROVEN ADVENTURE that gives FULFILLMENT, PRIDE, and SATISFACTION, even when we FAIL.

HAPPINESS is the JOURNEY! Not the destination. It is working and living with each other to defeat ENTROPY and its SPAWN, randomness, chaos, mutation, ignorance, bad data, misunderstanding, psychopathology, political corruption, BUSTED, and BULLSHIT, while CREATING survival and prosperity for our children.

17

FALSE TRUTH

IF our BELIEFS FAIL or are WRONG, yet we FIND enough INSPIRATION and FULFILLMENT in the PURSUING or RESULTS of the outcome to GIVE us peace of mind, then any failure is IRRELEVANT except to our children and loved ones who MUST INHERIT and SALVAGE OUT what we leave behind. And IF we LET THEM CHOOSE to live out their OWN DIFFERENT RELIGION or THEORY of life and cyberspace creations, NOTHING went WRONG. NO belief or person got BETRAYED and EVOLUTION CONTINUES as it always has because FOOLISHNESS or DECEPTION will be exposed or self-destruct by ENTROPY. FALSE BELIEFS lead to destruction.

However, our children MUST DIFFERENTIATE THEMSELVES FROM family and community beliefs and commitments to USE their own UNIQUE CHEMISTRY and LIFE EXPERIENCE for our species to BUILD the next BRIDGE over entropy, mutation, error, dysfunction, and change.

IT is EVERY PERSON'S INHERENT EVOLUTIONARY OBLIGATION to DEFINE their own IDENTITY and BELIEFS BECAUSE they are NOT FREE of their own controlling but UNKNOWN and UNPREDICTABLE cellular chemistry as their LIFE EXPERIENCE engages it. HOWEVER, it IS their LIFE'S MISSION to DISCOVER and ACT IT OUT.

THAT is our UNIQUE INHERITANCE no one CAN effectively PREDICT or DEFINE except ourselves AND NO ONE else has a RIGHT to TRY. How or what we DISCOVER in our STRUGGLE to live out its implications is WHAT EVOLUTION WINNOWS to make me and our species what we MUST BECOME for our FUTURE JUST LIKE ALL OUR ANCESTORS did.

EVOLUTION RULES

IT IS EVOLUTION that has GIVEN us OUR LIFE and we CANNOT ESCAPE the MECHANISM of death or its IMPLICATIONS and CONSEQUENCES. We MUST SERVE evolution because ENTROPY and MUTATION are the fundamental, inescapable conditions of the UNIVERSE that <u>MADE US</u> <u>POSSIBLE</u> and WINNOWING of MUTATION by EVOLUTION MUST remain the ultimate standard for predicting survival and prosperity.

INSTINCT

YET, PAIN, FEAR, hunger, fatigue, dysphoria, sex, pleasure, social interaction, and other INSTINCTIVE life experiences STIMULATE unconscious and conscious NEUROLOGICAL STATES such as attention, vigilance, remembering associating, expectations, emotions conditioned responses, homeostatic regulation, cognitive dissonance, sleep, and dreaming, to AUTOMATICALLY trigger hormones to INITIATE guide and sequence brain activity that results in UNCONSCIOUS processes and CONSCIOUS emotional experiences that stimulate, REWARD, and PUNISH, conscious behavior choices and mental ideation.

THIS CHEMICALLY DRIVEN EMOTIONAL and BEHAVIORAL INSTINCT AUTOMATICALLY ACTIVATES in our brain the SAME way EMPATHIC MIRROR NEURONS ACTIVATE to IMITATE/SIMULATE the central nervous system activation state of other PEOPLE who show the same body language and situational context we remember in ourselves. By recalling our FEELINGS in that context, we know THEIRS and thereby know whether their CHARACTER shows a GENUINE basis for a TRUSTING social relationship and effective SPECIES INTELLIGENCE.

NEURON CELL CHEMISTRY is a CONTINUUM of PROCESSES that INCLUDE diverse brain functions like recording of life experience as memory, instinctive emotions, intuitive behaviors, conscious self-awareness, problem solving, etc.

THEREFORE, our CONSCIOUS EXPERIENCE IS only the very SMALL TIP of an ICEBERG with an ENORMOUS UNCONSCIOUS mass (98 percent) that supports IT in the NUCLEUS of the cells in the NEURONAL NET of our brain and the difference between the "read only memory" in the single cell we begin life with and our TEMPORARY life experience memory is INCREDIBLY COMPLEX CHEMISTRY of cells so small we can NOT SEE.

More than that IT IS STILL NOT CLEAR IF HOW WE LIVE OUR LIVES gets PACKED into the UNCONSCIOUS CHEMISTRY of our CHILDREN through our GAMETES. It certainly would confer evolutionary advantage if we were successful in our life as well as a source of species diversity if we weren't.

INSTINCT IS a FORM of PREPROGRAMMED "CLASSICAL CONDITIONING" that USES the same chemistry that records LIFE EXPERIENCE, gets recognized by MIRROR NEURONS, and TRIGGERS CONSCIOUS AWARENESS of EMOTIONS, INSTINCTS, INTUITIONS, CONDITIONED LEARNING, and BEHAVIOR IMPULSES.

20

DEFENSE MECHANISMS

THIS chain of CHEMICAL causation is DESIGNED to GUIDE our CONSCIOUS INTELLECT to STRATEGIZE current behavior to SATISFY instinctive emotional WISDOM but is only as ADAPTIVE as EVOLUTION could make it and is corrupted by mutation and trauma or dysfunctional context.

SO, IF INTELLECT CANNOT fulfill or RESOLVE our emotions, COGNITIVE DISSONANCE TRIGGERS ANXIETY that FORCES our INTELLECT to OBSESS till our anxiety becomes so INTENSE and DYSPHORIC that we sometimes USE NEUROTIC DEFENSE MECHANISMS to SHUT IT DOWN by CREATING and JUSTIFYING DYSFUNCTIONAL BELIEF SYSTEMS that GIVE us PEACE OF MIND despite making us STUPID, defensive, and abusive.

THEREFORE, INADEQUATELY RESOLVED INSTINCTIVE EMOTION is the BREEDING GROUND for delusion, bias, failure, self-destruction, abuse, hate, crime, and insanity.

THEORIES, PREDICTIONS, and RELIGIONS CONCEIVED in association with common EMOTIONS like ambition, greed, lust, anxiety, frustration, anger, shame, fear, or envy, MUST be CONSTANTLY CONFRONTED for EXPERIMENTALLY VERIFIED FACT and TRUTH or the concepts we believe are TRUE become antisocial, abusive, depressed, or dysfunctional, in a QUEST for PEACE OF MIND.

AS EXAMPLES, CHRONIC ANGER makes us IRRITABLE and THINK others are VICTIMIZING us when they are NOT and we BROOD about what EVIL is doing this, or chronic FEAR makes us UNABLE to take any RISK, LASH OUT impulsively or act FOOLISHLY right when it is most important to act WISELY, or SHAME makes us GIVE UP our creative intelligence and believe ANYTHING social norms tell us, or DEPRESSION makes us THINK we are BAD people SO we self-destruct or SUBMIT to slavery, or social and sexual PREOCCUPATION convinces us others LOVE US, or want to VICTIMIZE us and causes BAD JUDGMENTS of other people's INTENTIONS, PERSONALITY, and INTELLIGENCE, or DYSFUNCTIONAL religions make us unable to do problem solving, or TRAUMA triggers REACTION FORMATION that makes us believe ANYTHING our victimizers say.

21

EMOTIONAL BIAS

SYMBOLS that our creative INTELLIGENCE USES to THINK with mostly ACQUIRE instinctive EMOTIONAL POWER in CHILDHOOD when ANCIENT cellular chemistry and care givers DOMINATE our IGNORANT brain and behavior with INSTINCT and FUSES EMOTION with every MEMORY of events, objects, interpretations, meaning, values, concepts, theories, belief systems, etc.

THIS is CLASSICAL PSYCHOLOGICAL CONDITIONING that uses cellular chemistry to FUSE EMOTION with EVERY memory just like PAVLOV'S dogs STARTED unconscious SALIVATING at the SOUND of a BELL if food had been previously presented at the SAME TIME. The sound and instinctive anticipation of food were unconsciously WELDED TOGETHER to make the sound AUTOMATICALLY trigger salivation the dog HAS NO CONTROL OVER.

IN FACT, like Pavlov's dogs it is the EMOTIONAL CONTENT of memories that neurons PRIMARILY use to sort, classify, record, and index, memories for access and retrieval by UNCONSCIOUS ASSOCIATIONS so the ones with NO emotional relevance GET FORGOTTEN as trivia while we sleep and it is the TRAIL of remembered emotions we FOLLOW when we THINK CREATIVELY about PROBLEMS that allows our SUBCONSCIOUS to BREAK

THROUGH any stalemated understanding/misunderstanding which locks up our conscious symbolic intellect.

CONVERSELY, we also genuinely religiously deeply BELIEVE and JUSTIFY misunderstandings, LIES, irrational theories, dysfunctional religions, or FLAGRANTLY FALSE assertions of fact to DEFEND EMOTIONAL CONVICTIONS.

THE WAY we CODE EMOTION into our scenarioizing and simulation of the real world is HOW the creative GOLDEN PATH gets the eye-popping COLOR that lets the most LIKELY SOLUTIONS to our creative challenges stand out among the IMPOSSIBLY MASSIVE NUMBER of POTENTIAL solutions hidden in the CREATIVELY alternative hypotheses we CAN SYMBOLICALLY construct in the FREEDOM of CYBERSPACE.

Otherwise the RATIONAL POSSIBILITIES and potential delusions OVERWHELM scenarioizing, simulating, and evaluating hypothesis to find the few we have time and resources to test by experiment.

SO, the SYMBOLS, beliefs, and religions we MATURE with or ACQUIRE as adults in reaction to EMOTIONAL IMPERATIVES like pain, fear, success, failure, dominance, love, shame, envy, hate, lust, hunger etc., ARE UNCONSCIOUSLY FUSED in our MEMORY with EMOTION by cellular chemistry that INTERPRETS, STRUCTURES, and BIASES our USE of those SYMBOLS. (Like visual icons, words, images, incidents, ideas, concepts, etc.)

It is this BIAS that makes it CRITICAL to our OBJECTIVE intelligence that we have a WISE RELIGION to INTERPRET and CONDITION instinctive emotions in our FIREWALL between the PASSION of instinct and the PREDICTIONS of OBJECTIVE intelligence.

22

OBSESSION

EACH RECALLED INCIDENT inevitably has SIMILARITIES in facts, circumstance, context, interpretation, associations, symbolism, meaning, theory, etc., to OTHER spontaneously recalled incidents that CONTAIN PREVIOUS SYMBOLIC INTERPRETATIONS that ALSO BRING their own conditioned EMOTIONS and SYMBOLIC expression with other RATIONAL INTERPRETATIONS, IMPLICATIONS, and EMOTIONAL IMPERATIVES.

EVERY SINGLE TIME an INCIDENT and its EMOTION is CONSCIOUSLY REMEMBERED, the paired classical conditioning GETS STRONGER and associations more ELABORATED SO the more EMOTIONALLY relevant parts of IT GET REINTERPRETED, REORGANIZED, and EMPHASIZED around the CURRENT emotional priorities. SO MEMORIES CHANGE or are repressed including the FUSED EMOTIONS and MEANING.

Subjective REALITY MUTATES and EVERYTHING must be subject to corroboration and review after each new mental experience. Comparing and contrasting new understanding against accepted fact and theories must be routine to objectively integrate them.

IDEAS can EVOLVE their meaning because they are SYMBOLIC and can FOLLOW a purely symbolic evolution and mental SIMULATION of causation processes that are programmable quite independently of our neuronal chemistry or the world around us just like computer programs process input and upgrade its own operating program.

SO conscious INTELLECT must FULLY mature an INTELLIGENT FIREWALL to STAND on its OWN BEFORE it CAN manage or CONTROL the DOMINANCE of instinctive emotions.

Luckily, the most highly intelligent, brilliant, genius level, insightful, creative, and complex concepts, can be created or CONCEIVED piecemeal in stair stepped STAGES of partial insight by PROGRESSIVE scenarioizing of simulations of the real world by ORDINARILY intelligent people or groups of people who WORK HARDER or longer to scenarioize and simulate more because they are more STRONGLY creatively MOTIVATED by PASSION, inspiration, love, obsession, religion, ambition, social relationships, compassion, fear, trauma, etc.

This book follows that plan but my rearrangement of old ideas with new interpretation will necessitate re-reading and REFLECTION to find application to YOUR LIFE. Re-reading creates a STRONG sensory memory for your IMAGINATION to LATER visualize the IDEAS and FEEL the EMOTIONS of CREATING NEW UNDERSTANDING about something you CARE about, and the long sentences CONNECT contingent conditional IDEAS in a single VISION to build overarching CONTEXT that may later become your beliefs. You will need to CONSCIOUSLY comprehend a LARGE section of your CYBERSPACE to INTELLIGENTLY and CREATIVELY REARRANGE OLD COMMON IDEAS like a picture puzzle USING RECOGNITION of relationships to put it ALL TOGETHER in CYBERSPACE.

An EXAMPLE of the PROGRESSIVE classical conditioning of intellect is when the associated good feelings of the sight, smell, body language, and behavior of your mother or care giver BECOMES recognizing and re-experiencing your nurturing HISTORY with them, food they cook, appearance, their speaking style, the MEANING and values they communicate, ideas, concepts, ideals, PURPOSE they follow with YOUR LOVING TRUST.

You DON'T HAVE to be a brilliant genius to be WISE about the most sophisticated, abstract, and complex TRUTH if you conceive it as successive parts of a WHOLE just the way a child evolves through academic education to GRADUATION, maturity, competence, self-reliance, and self-sufficiency.

A GOLDEN path of METAPHORS, ANALOGIES, and ASSOCIATIONS can be CREATED like stepping stones across a RIVER of RANDOM CHAOS that traces HIDDEN PATHWAYS of objective TRUTHS that RUN this universe.

CREATIVELY INTELLIGENT LIVING can be like an escalator powered by UNCONSCIOUS PASSION. It doesn't HAVE to FORCE concentration, be hyper-vigilant, or flash like lightening, because instinctive emotions are CHEMICAL and continuously PRODUCE NEURAL STIMULATION UNCONSCIOUSLY like a BATTERY. It is the UNDISCIPLINED power of instinctive emotion that CORRUPTS objective intelligence, NOT low IQ, or the SPEED of intellectual association. If you know the path you can follow it.

HOWEVER, WHEN there is TOO MUCH REHEARSAL of MEMORY, interpretation, or ideas, due to current EMOTIONAL IMPERATIVES or social conditioning from defensive anxiety, cognitive dissonance, religious obsession, or trauma, the EMBEDDED EMOTION further AMPLIFIES chemical processes for more INTENSE OBSESSION and COMPULSION that can PREVENT OBJECTIVE EVALUATION with thoughts that are DELUSIONAL BECAUSE the obsession is CUT OFF from external corroboration or validation by EMOTIONAL IMPERATIVES imposed by "SURVIVAL of the FITTEST" INSTINCTS like "fight or flight" and we CAN no longer THINK OBJECTIVELY.

23

DELUSIONS

THIS defensive reaction to UNRESOLVED instinctive emotions like fear, greed, hate, or infatuation can become a BLIND FAITH BELIEF SYSTEM DEFENDED by RATIONALIZATIONS which EXEMPT IT from corroboration, validation, intelligent analysis, or ANY REAL-WORLD ACCOUNTABILITY.

AN EXAMPLE of common delusion is IDEALISM, INFATUATION, FEAR, HATE, or RELIGION that becomes exaggerated and distorted by CONSCIOUS PANIC reactions to TRAUMA or self-interest, that can override creative intelligence with RIGID EMOTIONAL DEMANDS.

CELLULAR CHEMISTRY, INSTINCTIVE PERSONALITY, SITUATIONAL CONTEXT, and LIFE HISTORY PREDICT over 90 percent of what we FEEL, THINK, and DO, because we ARE chemical computers and they are our PROGRAM. SO, INTELLIGENCE just objectively FACILITATES INTEGRATION of EMOTIONS into a belief system, plans, and actions for objective ACHIEVEMENT of goals for survival and prosperity.

CELLULAR CHEMISTRY AUTOMATICALLY KEEPS CONTROL of living priorities mostly UNCONSCIOUS to keep our CONSCIOUS MIND from INTERFERING with our evolution designed AUTOMATIC CHEMICAL PROGRAMMING and

THE INTENSELY DISCIPLINED INTELLIGENT STRUGGLE of our LIVES is spent DISCOVERING, BALANCING, and INTEGRATING them into a conscious BELIEF SYSTEM that WORKS OUT our UNIQUE destiny the BEST way we CAN considering EVERYTHING in our UNIQUE life SO EVOLUTION can pick the WINNER that best serves the common and individual GOOD.

24

MENTAL MATURATION

Distributed SOCIAL CULTURE has a SERIOUS CHALLENGE to make appropriate RELIABLE interpretations of INSTINCTIVE EMOTIONS and intuition in individual children CONSIDERING the wide range of <u>CHILDREN'S</u> instinctive personality and social or religious MATURATION in their FAMILY of ORIGIN BECAUSE family, cultural, or public religious VALUES, or norms, can CONFLICT with childhood attempts to CONNECT UNIQUELY DIVERSE, undefined, unknown, and labile instinctive emotions to COMMUNITY INTELLECTUAL SYMBOLS, SOCIAL NORMS, or public RELIGION they have not been taught.

THE FAMILY or COMMUNITY may JUDGE, PUNISH, or TRAUMATIZE, a child's DIFFERENCES from the GENOMIC NORM enough to DISTURB, DISRUPT, DISORDER, and PATHOLOGIZE their intellectual, social, emotional, and religious MATURATION of a BELIEF SYSTEM.

AS AN ANALOGY of "learn by doing" is we may KNOW we are HUNGRY but NOT KNOW what FOOD would SATISFY the CRAVING SO we MUST CONSCIOUSLY CONSIDER a range of CHOICES of behaviors that may REQUIRE CREATIVITY in ACTING OUT impulses and TASTING the RESULTS to FIND the right recipe to SATISFY our taste discrimination and RISK failing or bad consequences.

CHILDREN and even adults may NOT KNOW what they INTUITIVELY WANT or WHY they YEARN for something different or discriminant BECAUSE the diversity of cellular chemistry or childhood abuse REQUIRES them to INVESTIGATE their cognitive dissonance, UNCONSCIOUS discontent, or dysphoria, and ACT OUT behaviors that RISK inappropriate or self-destructive CONSEQUENCES as part of FINDING OUT what their ancient homeostatic mental and social INSTINCTS WANT from them. Much juvenile delinquency and self-destructive adolescent REBELLION or dysfunction RESULTS from this.

THIS is especially TRUE of SEXUAL INSTINCTS but it APPLIES to ALL emotions including PSYCHOPATHIC sadism till we LEARN to MAKE BALANCED, consciously intelligent connections between our instinctive-emotional cellular chemistry and ADAPTIVELY APPROPRIATE, INTELLIGENT SOCIAL BEHAVIORS, through regulation by a creatively intelligent, consciously strategized, wise religion, and FIREWALL.

THIS is the PROCESS of MATURATION.

25

WINNOWING FOR INTELLIGENCE

SURPRISINGLY, the EVOLUTION of INTELLIGENCE and EMPATHY has been PRIMARILY DRIVEN by a CHEMICAL SUB-SET of HUMAN BEINGS with an obsessively SELF-SERVING instinctive cellular chemistry with the EMOTIONAL DRIVER of GREED and SADISTIC HATE right from the BEGINNING of our SPECIES that HAVE little or NO FEAR, EMPATHY, COMPASSION, or IDENTITY FUSION.

THESE PSYCHOPATHS are the GRIM REAPERS of EVOLUTION ARMED with BETRAYAL and BORN into OUR FAMILIES as brothers and sisters and often RAISED by PSYCHOPATHIC PARENTS who BECOME mothers and fathers by the ACT of SEX for THEIR OWN PERSONAL POWER or SADISM, who will never permit independence and ABUSIVELY CONTROL the personal SUCCESS and SUBMISSION of their children as objects of possession to be controlled, abused, or abandoned for their own satisfaction with their INVESTMENT.

THEY SURPRISE us BECAUSE they are INVISIBLY different from EMPATHICALLY LINKED people and VERY DIFFICULT to recognize due to often EMERGING out of LOVING PARENTS, BENIGN childhood INFLUENCES, or shared religious assertions, and DO NOT act on their genomic differences till their UNIQUE INSTINCTS create BELIEFS, emotional expression, and obsessions at

MATURITY and INDEPENDENCE gives them freedom of action but even then they may be BRILLIANT at hiding that nature behind sharply INSIGHTFUL INTELLIGENCE and ACTING.

PSYCHOPATHS ALSO can be created by CHILDHOOD ABUSE that has epigenetically REPROGRAMMED their neurological development with METHYLATION, PROTEOLYSIS, and chemical MUTATION DUE to REACTION FORMATION from TRAUMA or DEVELOPMENTAL DISRUPTION.

26

SPECIES LEVEL INTELLIGENCE

IN ANCIENT TIMES, psychopaths DROVE our PREDATION on EACH OTHER and made us EXTREMELY INTELLIGENT individually AND had OVERRIDING social INSTINCTS that made us easy to TRAUMATIZE into SLAVERY requiring sophisticated specialized TEAMWORK that CREATED an AGGREGATED GROUP INTELLIGENCE, LINKED by EMPATHY, compassion, identity fusion, shared experience, religion, social values, INSPIRATION, and NURTURING.

FEAR is our NORMAL life because it DRIVES us to WORK EVERY DAY— and always has from the beginning of time— to survive and STRUGGLE for prosperity. Yet, it makes us VERY SMART if we can learn to MANAGE our EMOTIONS of greed, anger, hate, revenge, depression, hopelessness, etc.

However, THESE OVERLORDS RULED EVOLUTION LIKE the GREEK GODS with guiltless, remorseless, ruthless manipulation, exploitation, predation, coercion, violence, deception, and murder, USING sharply insightful intelligence to coldly analyze the BEHAVIOR of everyone else and PREDICT their reactions so THEY could ACT in a totally PERSUASIVE manner to APPEAR intelligent, charismatic, charming, empathic, supernatural, inspirational, trustworthy, intimidating, and any other WONDERFUL or TERRIFYING way to MANIPULATE them to DO whatever they WANTED. They are PERFECT warlords, kings, nobility, CEO's, venture capitalists, entrepreneurs, salesmen, preachers, soldiers, assassins, criminals, thugs, bullies, and politicians.

ANYONE that would NOT SUBMIT was judged, manipulated, co-opted, slandered, persecuted, criminalized, terrorized, tortured, and murdered. They committed GENOCIDE to all REBELLION but RATIONALIZED IT as RIGHTEOUS BEHIND GOVERNMENT, BUSINESS, CHURCH, RELIGION, cults, or any other ORGANIZED POWER including family, and BEST friends.

THEY ORGANIZED sophisticated DEFACTO "SLAVE" societies BRED to be linked by cellular chemistry to form a SUPERIOR AGGREGATED INTELLIGENCE UNDER THEIR PERSONAL CONTROL much like the INTENT of the BUILDERS of SKY NET in *the TERMINATOR* movies, the BORG in *Star Trek*, VICKI in *I ROBOT*, and *THE MATRIX*.

Cesar built a bridge across the mile-wide Bosporus in two weeks, marched his fifty thousand-man army across, looked around and marched home as a AWESOME DEMONSTRATION of organization. The Persians stepped down from WAR till they had a million.

THESE DYNAMICS have been popular as MOVIES BECAUSE they HAVE ALREADY been USED by WARLORDS and OVERLORDS of our past to CREATE highly intelligent slave organizations LINKED by EMPATHY and identity fusion. That NIGHTMARE still haunts us even though THEIR CREATION of US to be intelligent domesticated servants resulted in us TURNING AGAINST them with SUPERIOR INTELLIGENCE.

COMMUNITY SELF-DEFENSE

HOWEVER, they are STILL strongly AMONG US in our species gene pool because their use of DECEPTION and RUTHLESSNESS continues to AGGREGATE POWER as money and ONLY the SMARTEST, best EDUCATED, and RICHEST of us CAN ESCAPE their PREDATION.

THEY CALL themselves real estate brokers, bankers, ENTREPRENEURS, venture capitalists, fiscal conservatives, and MINISTERS, but they are just OLD FASHIONED PREDATORS and PSYCHOPATHS who have CORNERED us UP using PRIVATION, POVERTY, CHILD ABUSE, WORK, RELIGION, bribery, seduction, ignorance, isolation, deception, trauma, technology, corruption, politics, rationalizations, SUPERIOR EDUCATION, and RECRUITMENT of BRILLIANT CONSULTANTS to STRATEGIZE their DECEPTIONS with fear, religion, rationalizations, distortion, distraction, scapegoating, slander, greed, envy, ambition, resentment, and hate.

PSYCHOPATH PARANOIA

Their HIGH DOLLAR PRIVACY SCREEN has PREVENTED us from seeing through their cover stories by CONSTANTLY BLAMING EVERYTHING on government workers and the rules they FOLLOW. (PARODY satire follows.) GOVERNMENT WORKERS deserve NO sympathy from ANYONE for the FORTUNE in TAXES THEY GIVE AWAY, in ways I QUESTION while I work two jobs and WORRY about my kids going to college. Government workers DESERVE BLAME for doing work NOBODY WANTS TO PAY FOR. They should be FIRED and let "SURVIVAL OF THE FITTEST" REIGN on EVERYONE. YOU THINK WE ARE AFRAID OF SHUTTING DOWN GOVERNMENT? WE HAVE LOTS OF GUNS. LET ARMAGEDDON BEGIN! We can LOOT what we need and hide out till SOMEONE gets EXTERMINATED. We have WAY TOO MANY people on this planet anyway. Life was BETTER in the old days when we could just go out there and KILL them or get KILLED and be MARTYRS and HEROES. However, THE ONES THAT ARE LEFT WILL BE RICH ENOUGH TO KEEP SLAVES! (End PARODY.)

NOW we are PARANOID that OUR GOVERNMENT or any AUTHORITY, CONTROL, or INTELLIGENCE greater than ours WILL TURN AGAINST US to exploit, corrupt, brutalize, enslave, terrorize, rob, or kill us as isolated helpless individuals UNABLE to FIGHT massive organization, technological POWER, and SUPERIOR INTELLIGENCE.

SOME of us have even BECOME LIBERTARIAN to ESCAPE that FEAR by BELIEVING in NO GOVERNMENT or religion at all DESPITE our obviously OVERWHELMING social INSTINCTS to care about and RELATE to each other through FAMILY, CHILDHOOD FRIENDS, ADULT PARTNERSHIPS, culture, shared experience, self-interest, education, values, personality compatibility beliefs, religion, obsessions, inspirations, goals, creativity, infatuation, love, and identity fusion, to say NOTHING about being able to WORK FOR A LIVING.

These people connections WILL GUARANTEE intense struggle WITHOUT government protection but WITH unrestricted theft, coercion, victimizing, violence, and death. Even just one other person makes a COMMUNITY with MUTUAL OBLIGATIONS that WILL be violated without democratic political control.

Psychopaths learned to FAKE and MANIPULATE ALL THAT politics by watching us struggle to satisfy emotional imperatives but without feeling ANYTHING themselves. This gave them intelligent OBJECTIVITY so they can see what WORKS without the SELF-DECEPTION of emotional IMPERATIVES imposed on empathic and compassionate people by their own cellular chemistry and their culture.

PSYCHOPATHS even EXPLOIT this PARANOIA by preemptively BLAMING our GOVERNMENT to HIDE their own VICTIMIZING and USE our FEAR against us by OFFERING SAFETY with the BAIT of RATIONALIZATIONS, RELIGION, PATRIOTISM, AUTHORITY, MONEY, SOCIAL RANK, flattery, rewards, promotions, threats, promises, co-opting, corruption, or hate with great acting that appeals to our unconscious instincts.

THEY OFFER UTOPIAN SOCIETIES like SOCIALISM, FREE MARKET CAPITALISM, MILITARY CULTISM, HERO WORSHIP, or RELIGION, but when we TAKE the deal it IS NOT what we THOUGHT before the TRAP SNAPPED and IT IS TOO LATE for DEMOCRATIC control. They are brilliant CONS.

The FOUNDING fathers of the United States KNEW to be PARANOID about the CORRUPTION of POWER when they wrote its CONSTITUTION to include three counter-balancing power sources. They knew power attracts CORRUPTION and the more POWER, the BIGGER the SWARM of SMARTER, more DECEPTIVE psychopaths that CAUSE then CO-OPT our problems, to offer HELP that makes us SLAVES to their CONTROL.

THE BRAVE NEW WORLD of the future CAN BE SUCCESSFULLY RUN by PSYCHOPATHS just like the COMMUNISTS, FASCISTS, and NAZIS have ALREADY PROVEN. They ALWAYS SUCCEED until their NARCISSISM and SADISM BLINDS their objectivity and ENTROPY forces us to socially AGGREGATE with EMPATHY and refuse to believe their DECEPTIONS.

Their trick is to create IRRELEVANT ISSUES that appeal to our emotions so we believe OTHER, fear mongering or greedy deceptions that gives them power using anger, fear, hate, and greed to create a RELIGION to BLIND US. They SLANDER the UNIFYING NURTURING power of EMPATHY, altruism, conscience, compassion, and the SUPERIOR SPECIES INTELLIGENCE it CREATES.

They are UNWILLING to PAY for the COMPASSION WE FEEL when innocents SUFFER, so they PUMP UP THE HATE, to save the money.

CRIMINALS

Psychopaths have ALWAYS been with us and always WILL be if the DIVERSITY of INSTINCT leaves some children WITHOUT fear, empathy, identity fusion, or compassion, and LEAVES SADISM, INTELLIGENCE, and EGOTISM.

However, the larger society NEEDS to believe in a future without victimizing to JUSTIFY their own DAILY SACRIFICE to the common good, believing in social EQUALITY, and TRUST that others will respect the SAFETY of ALL our DREAMS.

Therefore, the EVOLUTIONARY WINNOWING of CELL LINES MUST CONTINUE because our children MUST BE PROTECTED, TAUGHT, and RESOURCED with our highest intelligence and wisdom because they must live democratically with people believing DIFFERENTLY from them but still work TOGETHER to set goals and resolve conflicts, without victimizing, humiliating, lying, BETRAYING, or deceiving.

Yet, the intelligence of the EMPATHIC MAJORITY is OBJECTIVELY COMPROMISED by the CONFLICT of EMPATHY with REVENGE SO the JUSTICE of ENFORCEMENT should NOT be PUT in public CONTROL.

WHAT TO DO WITH CRIMINALS

CITIZENS who support the COMMON GOOD of SPECIES INTELLIGENCE have a RIGHT to PROTECT THEMSELVES from self-serving psychopaths who STILL live by the rule of selfish genes and hate.

CRIMINALS NEED to be SEGREGATED where they cannot HARM COMMUNITY members or their activities BUT they CAN CONTINUE to follow their abusive PSYCHOPATHOLOGY, CELLULAR CHEMISTRY, VICTIMIZING HISTORY, criminal INTENT, victimizing CHOICES, and rationalizing BELIEFS, but also NOT be protected from the consequences of their own behavior and belief in a segregated community of "DEFIANCE" where they will succeed or fail without PUBLIC resource or rescue. The goal of segregation is not punishment, revenge, or rehabilitation. It is to LET THEM CREATE a separate lifestyle of their own CHOOSING when they use ours to victimize US.

PSYCHOPATHS AS VICTIMS

Psychopaths may GROW UP NORMALLY with their evil potential completely unconscious like everyone else, then an INCIDENT or temptation makes them suddenly NOTICE they are DIFFERENT from most people because they are free from emotional COMPULSIONS like fear, empathy, or compassion, that control other people, and the INSIGHT RADICALIZES them with an EPIPHANY that excites their ANALYTICAL WORLD with their OPPORTUNITY to possess and DO anything they WANT, WITHOUT REMORSE, to fill their aloneness and EMPTINESS or take REVENGE on innocents for the ECSTASY of HATE REVENGE.

OR their CELLULAR CHEMISTRY just MATURES and they casually WONDER why the people they learn to PREDICT, BUILD relationships with, MANIPULATE, and DOMINATE, seem to have GENUINE AFFECTION with each other when THEY FEEL NOTHING SO they may DO RESEARCH or TEST themselves in INTENSE social interaction to see if they CAN provoke EMPATHIC social FEELINGS in themselves and manipulate others to show FEELINGS in response. They may study acting and are KEEN observers who KEEP THE SCORE.

THEY may ANALYTICALLY WONDER IF they are just naturally inhibited, constitutionally phlegmatic, or depressed, and some investigate mental disorders to discover they are PSYCHOPATHS but there IS NOTHING they CAN DO or ultimately CARE about except to SHARPEN their ambition and victimizing. This kind is too smart and disciplined to get caught once they KNOW THE SCORE.

THEY even get married, MAKE BABIES, and PERFORM SUPERFICIALLY PERSUASIVE family rituals that even fool spouses but they ARE just EMPTY of EMOTION except for NARCISSISM, selfish ambition, hate, and revenge NO MATTER what they DO.

However, their children BECOME POWER OBJECTS they selfishly and sadistically CONTROL, punish, or abandon, if they do NOT become useful, powerful, or SUBMIT.

SELF DEFENSE BY PSYCHOPATHS

HOWEVER, they DO LEARN to ACT like they FEEL exemplary social PASSION, DEEP BELIEFS, or RELIGIOUS PASSION, and they LEARN with great analytical observation and insight BECAUSE they are NOT DISTRACTED by compassion, conscience identity fusion, aggregation of species intelligence, derivative social norms, democratic community management, or other instinctive social or religious emotion. SO, they PRECOCIOUSLY TEACH themselves to SUPERFICIALLY ACT charismatic and charming to become LEADERS by ACTING while retaining their RUTHLESS OPPORTUNISM and SADISTIC SATISFACTIONS.

YET, they ENVY and ARE MYSTIFIED by the INSTINCTIVE COMPASSION, identity fusion, empathy, mothering, social selflessness, affection, religious beliefs, and infatuation driven identity fusion EMPATHIC people HAVE with each other.

Much LATER in their emotional evolution and POWER they WILL TAKE REVENGE on INNOCENTS with that ENVY to PROVE themselves SUPERIOR to the COMPASSIONATE emotions of EMPATHIC people and take REVENGE for being REJECTED over their sadism.

PSYCHOPATHIC DOMINANCE

ULTIMATELY, they GENUINELY BELIEVE their ABILITY to TAKE LEADERSHIP and inflict suffering without conscience IS an ACHIEVEMENT of their INTELLIGENCE according to the RULES of the GAME of life or a GIFT from GOD to punish and control us on HIS behalf with SELF RIGHTEOUS ZEAL.

They WILL BELIEVE ANY rationalization for SADISM like PATRIOTISM, RACE, RELIGION, GOVERNMENT, or ECONOMIC THEORY, the same way WE BELIEVE OUR rationalizations. ALL HUMANS GENUINELY justify their emotions unless they become OBJECTIVE. That is the evolved PURPOSE of creative intelligence. That is why we MUST LEARN OBJECTIVITY.

SOCIAL RECOGNITION, academic credentials, education, training, and ANOINTMENT by CHURCHES feeds their NARCISSISM and MAKES them SELF-RIGHTEOUS and UNTOUCHABLE by reason, science, common sense, knowledge, culture, tradition, compassion, infatuation, lovers, or fear, and they BECOME ARROGANT self-aggrandizing leaders or teachers and the center of PERSONALITY CULTS or RELIGIOUS ORGANIZATIONS and deeply believe they DESERVE to be WORSHIPED and control or destroy the lives of other people. These are called NARCISSISTS because they DEEPLY BELIEVE they are ALWAYS RIGHT.

HOWEVER, IF WE were LUCKY enough for THEM to be BORN into LOVING families who use prosocial conditioning with education and resources or they ARE NOT very far into the chemical causes of psychopathy, they may NEVER BE TEMPTED to DO MORE than be socially abusive, DO petty criminal acts, or commit CHARACTER ASSASSINATIONS BECAUSE they can legitimately meet all their needs, use EFFECTIVE insight about BEHAVIOR, can ACCESS all the POWER they need, and are TOO SMART to VICTIMIZE in a way that might GET CAUGHT or compromise their social power base.

However, WE have only to WAIT for something like trauma, temptation, fanatical, social or religious movements, or catastrophic social challenge to RADICALIZE them and RELEASE the MONSTER INSIDE.

MANY quickly BECOME CRIMINALS and some BECOME SUICIDE BOMBERS or mass or serial murderers, BECAUSE they WERE ABUSED, TRAUMATIZED, socially isolated, or DID NOT RECEIVE COMPENSATORY empathic emotional conditioning as children.

PSYCHOPATHIC BLINDNESS

HOWEVER, when very HIGH FUNCTIONING PSYCHOPATHS GET SOCIAL POWER, none of them no matter how well BRED, SMART, or educated, can FULLY predict the consequences of VICTIMIZING BECAUSE they CANNOT understand the ultimate consequences of fear, trauma, and social betrayal on HIGHER emotional and social aggregated intelligence due to NOT having FEAR, compassion, or identity fusion themselves that would let them accurately predict the INSTINCTIVE FUTURE of our AGGREGATED species and whatever empathy their cellular chemistry develops is TRIMMED in adolescence BECAUSE they DON'T LIVE by IT.

THEIR NARCISSISM and EMPATHETIC BLINDNESS makes them UNDERESTIMATE everyone else and ESPECIALLY SPECIES LEVEL AGGREGATED INTELLIGENCE SO they are INSIDIOUSLY DANGEROUS POLITICIANS like POL POT, STALIN, MAO TSE TUNG, and HITLER, who became godlike.

Psychopaths are INCORRIGIBLE, CONGENITAL HATERS, and it HAS NOTHING AT ALL to DO with their VICTIMS DESPITE ALL their BLAMING, justifications, rationalizations, and DECEPTIONS. Their RIGHTEOUSNESS is about their own CHARACTER of NARCISSISM, GREED, deception, sadism, and hate; anything can be their excuse for HATE but they just LIKE it.

TRAUMATIC OBSESSION COMPULSION

TO MAINTAIN their TERROR, PSYCHOPATHS FANTASIZE about and COMMIT gratuitous ATROCITIES to REHEARSE their PLEASURE from REVENGE and to PERFECT their control of the paralysis and SUBMISSION caused by FEAR and TERROR, imposed on EMPATHIC PEOPLE by HORROR.

THEY LIVE for the ECSTASY of BLOODLUST for innocents and GLORY in our TERROR when we are SEIZED by FEAR, CRUSHED by TRAUMA, and FRIED by PAIN. They line up at bloody car wrecks or disasters and have endless VICARIOUS questions about how the victims FEEL while they DRAMATIZE their LYING concern and ACT sympathetic.

BEHAVIORS that EVOLVE out of TRAUMAS CHEMICALLY IMPOSE OBSESSIONS, COMPULSIONS, PHOBIAS, clinical depression, psychosis, mental disorders, panic attacks, delusions, stress confusion, masochism, sadism, fugues, hate, bigotry, etc., to GUARANTEE our SURVIVAL with instinctive COMPULSIONS SO they WILL NOT STOP no matter how HARD our common sense or creative intelligence tries to discriminate, differentiate, and adapt to specific DYSFUNCTION.

THEREFORE COMPULSIONS, OBSESSIONS, DEPRESSION, ANXIETY, violence, hyperactivity, delusions, addictions, sexual lust, and PHOBIAS are MEDICATED by doctors, alcohol, ILLEGAL DRUGS or DISTRACTED by social organizations activism, politics, charities, rituals, sports, hobbies, games, religion, SEX, reading, television, or intellectual obsessions.

36

DELUSIONS

IF INTENSE THREAT or physical PAIN is PAIRED with emotional and RATIONALIZING DISINFORMATION, deception, indoctrination, brain washing, social immersion, social norm enforcement, or abusive religious dogma, DELUSIONAL neurotic IDEAS are PERMANENTLY preserved in neuronal circuitry with classical conditioning and ANCHORED by intellectual interpretation of life experience TOO cognitively DEFENDED for desensitization and cognitive reinterpretation to CHANGE. This includes organized BIGOTRY like racial, religious, and SEXUAL.

WE are INSTINCTIVELY PROGRAMMED to HOLD our BELIEFS, OBSESSIONS, and RATIONALIZATIONS as though our LIFE depends on it even when they are SELF-DESTRUCTIVE or SUICIDAL if they were learned in great EMOTIONAL pain and the SMARTER we ARE the MORE SYMBOLIC, ELABORATE, RESILIENT, and STUBBORN our NEUROTIC OBSESSION gets unless it becomes OBJECTIVE by DECONDITIONING emotion.

IF there IS CONTINUING HIGH STRESS life experience full of SYMBOLIC associations that TRIGGER frequent EMOTIONAL FLASHBACKS with MEMORIES of TRAUMATIC incidents that are associated with OVERWHELMING PHYSICAL SHOCK, the OBJECTIVITY of ONGOING intellectual judgments will be COMPROMISED by EMOTIONAL prioritizing and

INTERPRETATION which causes MORE failure triggered trauma that DEEPENS further into PERMANENT reaction formation, fanaticism, alcoholism, drug addiction, profound emotional withdrawal, suicide, or psychotic break with REALITY.

THE DEEPEST RELIGIOUS CONVICTIONS, inspiration, and strong intellectual beliefs MUST SUBMIT to this BRAIN WASHING or "breaking" by torture and psychological trauma ESPECIALLY if IT is IMPOSED on the ENTIRE society the way Communism was in the USSR, China, and Cambodia, or Nazism was in Germany before and during World War II or Bushido was in Japan.

THIS VULNERABILITY IS the MECHANISM that LET us SURVIVE as SLAVES in ancient times and even ADOPT the VALUES of our victimizers to BECOME their ZEALOUS slaves, functionaries, and soldiers. IT is sometimes currently called the "Stockholm Syndrome" when kidnap and torture VICTIMS fanatically JOIN their VICTIMIZERS.

THE VULNERABILITY is still PRESERVED in our CELLULAR CHEMISTRY BECAUSE IDENTITY FUSION still SERVES FAMILY and SPECIES emotional CONDITIONING. SO, WE can socially AGGREGATE at ANY COST.

SALVATION

HOWEVER, IF we DO decondition enough emotion from our intellect for it to become OBJECTIVE, we become more accurate in our predictions and gained problem solving skills from ADAPTING out of and TRANSCENDING the PRISON of IGNORANCE by using objective CREATIVE INTELLIGENCE to DESIGN a personal RELIGION able to nurture OBJECTIVITY while giving us FREEDOM to <u>CREATE</u> anything we can IMAGINE in OUR personal CYBERSPACE.

CHURCHES and ORGANIZED RELIGIONS did NOT and DO NOT CREATE or SPREAD the GOSPEL of TOLERANCE, EMPATHY, LOVE, and COMPASSION. They just ORGANIZE the social consequences of EMPATHY, compassion, identity fusion, OVERCOMING TRAUMA, and ORGANIZING aggregated community intelligence.

Yet, they inevitably <u>CORRUPT</u> IT in their DOGMA, FAITH, and ORGANIZATION by allowing PSYCHOPATHS to MANIPULATE themselves into the church POWER structure where they <u>MANIPULATE</u> and CORRUPT the CONCEPT of LITERAL BIBLE TRUTH, MIRACLES, HOLINESS, SACRED, SALVATION, ANOINTED, WORSHIP, OBEDIENCE, and the "HOLY SPIRIT" to give themselves power to INTERPRET and CONTROL the ORGANIZATION and ITS BELIEVERS the way the Catholic church and fundamentalist cult religions DO.

LIVING WITH PSYCHOPATHS

YET, PSYCHOPATHS DID NOT CHOOSE to be <u>EVIL</u>.

THEY HAD NO CHOICE BECAUSE CELLULAR CHEMISTRY DEFINES them just like the REST of US and their life experiences DO NOT and CANNOT give them the CHEMISTRY of FEAR, empathy, compassion, conscience, or aggregated species intelligence.

THEREFORE, CHANGING adults or "crystalized" personalities with LOVE, education, COUNSELING, therapy, reward, punishment or revenge is irrelevant, ineffective, wasteful, pointless, and HOPELESS except with their GENUINE OVERRIDING INTENT to CHANGE their OWN brain chemistry at ANY COST BECAUSE they can self-righteously <u>FAKE</u> inspiration, epiphany, transcendence, and religious salvation EASILY, with the cellular chemistry of DESPERATE OPPORTUNISM and dissociative ACTING that MAKES them <u>BELIEVE IT at the TIME</u> just like NARCISSISTS, egotists, sexual abusers, sadists, and drug addicts, BECAUSE IT GETS them what they WANT at ANY cost.

MANY of us still ACT OUT that HUMAN NATURE BECAUSE IT is STILL in our specie's cellular processes and our aggregated species intelligence must <u>STILL</u> FIND the WISDOM and STRATEGY to MANAGE THEM.

THEY NEED LIFESTYLES that CAN CONTRIBUTE to the COMMUNITY WITHOUT empathy, compassion, or remorse, but which LIMITS EGOTISM, SADISM, VICTIMIZING, or socialized HATE such as carefully organized and SUPERVISED APPLICATION jobs like technology, engineering, science, military, or police, where their normal intelligence, LACK of FEAR, and GOOD, OPPORTUNISTIC, goal driven INSIGHT into CONFUSION and MANIPULATION can be UTILIZED.

They make GREAT soldiers, policemen, assassins, double agents, secret agents, saboteurs, dictators, and traitors and GENUINELY BELIEVE they are PATRIOTS and SAINTS despite being ruthlessly self-centered and self-serving.

They EXCEL at OBSESSIVE-COMPULSIVE careers because they can NARROWLY FOCUS their intellect BETTER without global perspective or empathically linked social concerns just like some people with ASPERGER syndrome become SAVANT.

PSYCHOPATHS SHOULD BE KEPT OUT of POLITICS, LAW, RELIGION, TEACHING, PARENTHOOD, and the SOCIAL POWER of WEALTH.

39

INSTINCT WINS

THE GREAT POWER of creative intelligence is its INDEPENDENCE from OVERWHELMING INSTINCT BECAUSE OBJECTIVITY creates TRUE SIMULATION of REALITY that makes RELIABLE predictions of the future by being COLD and INDIFFERENT to the BIAS of EMOTION, instinct, and dysfunctional religion.

HOWEVER, THAT is also ITS GREAT WEAKNESS BECAUSE OBJECTIVE intelligence is free of emotions and does NOT CARE about ANYTHING including WORK, FIGHTING for SURVIVAL, self-interest, instinct, religion, or BEING CREATIVE, and HAS NO passion for PURPOSE to set priorities.

OBJECTIVITY GIVES UP and DIES in the challenge of FIGHTING for LIFE the way evolution requires; SO, the ULTIMATE PURPOSE of EVOLUTION, instinctive emotions religion, and creative intelligence must be our PASSION for SURVIVING and CREATING AT ANY COST.

We can CHOOSE our BELIEF SYSTEM in CYBERSPACE where our FIREWALL and religious self-conditioning can keep the overwhelming power of TRAUMA, instinct, chemical mutation, and emotional entropy BLOCKED from CORRUPTING the OBJECTIVITY of our creative symbolic intelligence but WE have to build the FIREWALL that holds back ENTROPY using CREATIVE INTELLIGENCE in our personal CYBERSPACE.

Yet, INSTINCTIVE EMOTIONS like infatuation are our ULTIMATE POWER SOURCE for giving purpose, prioritizing, and DRIVING survival and prosperity through self-conditioning. Emotions are like the lithium batteries that MUST be kept in a FIREPROOF box to SAFELY POWER the COMPUTER ASSISTED "fly by wire" controls of the enormous "Dreamliner" aircraft that can transport six hundred of us like life-giving blood cells to our life-affirming destinations.

Submitting to instinct is INESCAPABLE because EVOLUTION CREATED US and our LIFE EXPERIENCE is CHEMICALLY DRIVEN. SO, our FIREWALL must BALANCE instinctive UNCONSCIOUS neurological functions using religious self-conditioning to guide creative intelligence to THEORIZE a conscious BELIEF SYSTEM, interpret it, and act on it for survival, creativity, and prosperity. SO, strict OBJECTIVITY of FACT and IMPLICATIONS is NOT POSSIBLE or DESIRABLE. We are inherently SUBJECTIVE. However, our CREATIVE INTELLIGENCE can fly free out of THIS universe to create our own CYBERSPACE.

INTELLIGENCE is like a genie in a bottle that only GRANTS some WISHES but is NOT free to SERVE its own purpose or like a ROBOT programmed only to SERVE the arbitrary WHIM of its operator, SENSIBLE or NOT. That is why the warlords and overlords of our past believed they could create a superior intelligence they could CONTROL.

40

EMPATHY LIFELINE

HOWEVER, even UNWANTED, MALADAPTIVE, or SADISTIC, instinctive emotions are STILL ESSENTIAL to the next stage of ENHANCING SPECIES intelligence BECAUSE our own emotional reactions EMPOWER us to RECOGNIZE and know WHAT OTHER PEOPLE are FEELING and THINKING, BECAUSE we RE-EXPERIENCE the EMOTIONS of having the SAME behavior during OUR MATURATION or remember the same social context with people showing the same emotions and ultimate behavior which we can IMAGINE feeling CLOSE to. The emotional context helps us REMEMBER MEANING and PURPOSE.

THEREFORE, we can IMAGINE people's PERSONALITY to predict their INSTINCTIVE emotions, interpretations, symbolizing, and intentions to anticipate the OPTIMUM LANGUAGE or method to COMMUNICATE and PERSUADE complex ideas to them and UNDERSTAND theirs more accurately using METAPHORS, ANALOGIES, IMAGES, ASSOCIATIONS, DESCRIPTIONS, STORIES, and PARABLES that symbolize interpretations, meaning, concepts, ideas, religious precepts, scenarios, simulations, and strategies of cause, effect, and context.

THAT RICHNESS of THOUGHT ALLOWS us to SYMBOLICALLY communicate, analyze, hypothesize, ORGANIZE, coordinate, teach, negotiate, and think to CREATE interpersonal RELATIONSHIPS at a

SPECIES LEVEL to CONSTITUTE the aggregated INTELLIGENCE and functioning of our government, culture, and civilization, using social relationships, politics, religions, and institutions EVEN though these are prime power TARGETS of PSYCHOPATHS and subject to their CORRUPTION with BRILLIANT CO-OPTING, DECEPTION, and DIVERSION of resources and POWER, or hate TARGETING.

41

EMPATHIC DISCORD

YET, EMPATHY also INJECTS the discord, conflict, and CHAOS, of EXPERIENCING the inner processes of instinctive emotion, intellectual beliefs, and conflicts of OTHER people into our own UNIQUE STRUGGLE to self-manage and think creatively/intelligently.

Empathy emotionally CONDITIONS us to people, events, ideas, concepts, perspectives, religions, etc. that include TRAUMA, SUFFERING, and SADISM that DRIVES COGNITIVE DISSONANCE and CONFLICT which <u>CANNOT</u> be resolved. SO, we must be able to EMOTIONALLY <u>DETACH</u> from these FLASHBACKS or they will trigger OBSESSION-COMPULSION in us that can CRIPPLE our objective intellect and homeostatic emotional regulation with OVERRIDING survival INSTINCTS. This is PTSD.

We NEED the RUTHLESSNESS of SADISM to STAND GUARD over our CHEMICALLY DRIVEN EMPATHY, COMPASSION, RELIGION, and LOVE or we risk breakdown of OBJECTIVE creative intelligence and our ABILITY to SUCCEED AFTER we fail.

At a CERTAIN point in the CAUSATION and CONSEQUENCES of TRAUMA we must be able to CUT AWAY what we LOVE and believe in to save our own life and use the CLASSICAL CONDITIONING of SADISM and HATE to do it. So, we must have it available but safely secured by our PERSONAL RELIGION in our FIREWALL for the

ULTIMATE FIGHT or FLIGHT crisis to save our soul for OUR CHILDREN. Even HATE has its PURPOSE.

SO, EMPATHY is CLEARLY a SIGNIFICANT PROBLEM as well as the BLESSING of UNLIMITED aggregated species intelligence that REQUIRES a very intelligently designed DEFENSIVE PERSONAL FIREWALL for our own individual SAFETY and optimal OBJECTIVE intelligence but still allows beneficial PARTICIPATION in the AGGREGATED INTELLIGENCE of our SOCIETY as a WHOLE.

The many DANGERS and THREATS to ACTUALIZING EMPATHY means many people FAIL or evolve DISTORTED, BIASED, and DYSFUNCTIONAL, empathic ability particularly if they are ABUSED or DEPRIVED as children, have dysfunctional brain chemistry, have a belief system or religion based on submission, guilt, fear, blame, hate, or have limited DYSFUNCTIONAL SOCIAL EXPERIENCES.

42

FAMILY

IT is the CONDITIONED EMOTIONAL COMPONENT of SYMBOLS of OUR COMMUNITY ROLE that REWARDS, conditions, educates, or PUNISHES the behavior and work we MUST DO to receive the BENEFITS of aggregated intelligence, community organization, and religion. SO, it is <u>CRITICAL</u> that the symbols of our social and work life STRONGLY and positively reward appropriate adaptation or correct dysfunction to GIVE us SATISFACTION, FULFILLMENT, or guidance to CONSTRUCTIVELY PARTICIPATE in our community.

THIS is one RESPONSIBILITY of a partnership between PERSONAL and PUBLIC RELIGION.

SINCE the UNPREDICTABLY DIVERSE CELLULAR CHEMISTRY of every HUMAN PREDICATES interpretation of life experience, a WIDELY DIVERSE life experience, self-reflection, religious experience, and education is NECESSARY to allow EACH CHILD to FIND APPROPRIATELY DIFFERENTIATED and emotionally conditioned SYMBOLS for their unique PERSONALITY. They must DESIGN an adaptively intelligent personal religion to STRATEGIZE conditioning of their emotions to the symbols of their CHOSEN element of the community at LARGE.

THEREFORE, it is the ROLE of CARE GIVERS and the FAMILY of origin to PROVIDE emotional, social, intellectual, problem solving CONDITIONING at each DEVELOPMENTAL stage during the MATURATION of the unique cellular driven instincts of EACH of its children to the SYMBOLS of their currently anticipated FUTURE life DESPITE the FACT that their UNIQUE instinctive cellular chemistry is UNKNOWN and UNPREDICTABLE and may change or EVOLVE from what is APPARENT because it is subject to the RANDOM CONSEQUENCES of entropy and mutation on RECOMBINANT genetic and epigenetic chemical processes which we have no way to measure or control.

SO, a WIDE RANGE of DIVERSE conditioning opportunities must be PROVIDED and GUIDED SELF-SELECTION encouraged, organized, and NURTURED within families by CARE GIVERS.

IF the CARE GIVERS and FAMILY do NOT STRATEGIZE, guide, and PROVIDE appropriate life experience to condition the child's self-chosen instinctive potential to nurture them to create a personal religion, it may NEVER be REALIZED and DEFACTO become attached to ANTISOCIAL EMOTIONS like hopelessness, depression, apathy, bigotry, hate, sadism, greed, crime, compulsion, phobia, trauma, deception, blind rebellion, alcoholism, drug addiction, etc.

YET, DESPITE this PRIMARY ROLE of the FAMILY, WE EACH MUST DIFFERENTIATE OURSELVES from our family of origin when we MATURE into adulthood to FULFILL our UNIQUE creatively intelligent POTENTIAL to MAKE our own CREATIVE CONTRIBUTION to the community at large. Our family of origin CANNOT predict or control this.

NONE of us are CANNON FODDER, SLAVES, or ROBOTS whose only PURPOSE is to BE EXPENDED in SERVICE to religion, care givers, family, or community priorities.

Our evolutionary design dictates that the FUNCTION of the ADULT must be true to its cellular chemistry FIRST, then its unique interpretation of life experience, then its OWN chosen elements of the community at large, NOT other MEMBERS of the family of ORIGIN or their commitments, struggle, religion, or value system, despite what PSYCHOPATHIC PARENTS or other family members may DEMAND to make us SLAVES to THEIR NEEDS or EGOS.

However, this is destructive because unpredictable DIVERSITY is the inescapable evolutionary inheritance of entropy, mutation, and survival of our species, so any PERSONALITY TYPE may emerge from genetically recombinant cellular chemistry.

This DIVERSITY is PRECIOUS because its blessings cannot be predicted or trained but we can RECRUIT whatever sort of PERSON we NEED. The random chaos of evolution guarantees the BEST PERSON is in our specie's gene pool if we can find them to lead us ALL to escape the tyranny of ENTROPY and rigid cellular chemistry. The UNLIKELIEST or most deviant differentiation may be the ONE necessary to overcome our next specie's THREAT to survival and prosperity.

IT is the CHALLENGE of the CARE GIVERS of our FAMILY of ORIGIN that the EMOTIONAL conditioning of their children STRENGTHEN the child's UNIQUE instinctive cellular chemistry to BEST contribute to the aggregated community NEEDS BUT when the children reach MATURITY the family INFLUENCE MUST DETACH from them to ALLOW the new ADULT to DIFFERENTIATE HIM OR HERSELF from the common family and community commitments, concerns, values, and beliefs, to allow them COMPLETE INDEPENDENCE of JUDGMENT and ACTION SO that their UNIQUE personality can TAKE FULL RESPONSIBILITY to discern, differentiate, discriminate, and CREATE their OWN idea of their ROLE in society, personal religion, and WORK.

43

POVERTY AND BIGOTRY

IF the CARE GIVERS of the FAMILY of ORIGIN do NOT HAVE the RESOURCES or FREEDOM to PROVIDE the WIDE RANGE of education, training, and emotional conditioning the diverse cellular chemistry their children MAY NEED, their CHILDREN will be UNABLE to COMPETE in the community and FORCED to become socially DEVIANT and CRIMINAL to SURVIVE and will USE their INTELLIGENCE to REBEL against the aggregated intelligence of the community.

THEY will FORM CRIMINAL communal relationships with ANTISOCIAL VALUES that CONDITION their children to BECOME very smart PREDATORS and VICTIMIZERS READY to make their SUFFERING SERVE their deviant belief system and HATE for mainstream society and even CHOOSE to suffer and DIE in RECKLESS REBELLION using the SAME creatively intelligent cellular chemistry that HELPS the MAINSTREAM children SUCCEED and be GLORIFIED as HEROES. This is the ALT-RIGHT.

PUNISHMENT, REWARD, or OPERANT CONDITIONING by MAINSTREAM society will be USELESS because HATE MAKES aggregated community CONTROL of CREATIVE INTELLIGENCE GASOLINE on the FIRE.

Intelligence serves hate MORE easily than it serves EMPATHY because it is OBJECTIVE and does NOT CARE what purpose it serves. Hate makes the insight of intelligence relatively simple because it is NOT DISTRACTED by the GREAT COMPLEXITY of AGGREGATING the DIVERSITY of other people or society as a whole. THAT is why and how psychopaths controlled us for so LONG and why they are still our PRIMARY THREAT by using manipulative deception to co-opt and commandeer social power NOW with super computers and the SCIENCE of DEMOGRAPHICS.

UNFUSING EMOTION

Scenarios and simulations that TEST STRATEGIES for problem resolution must be FREE of emotional BIAS or creative symbolic intelligence are NOT OBJECTIVE and therefore <u>CONFOUNDED</u> and wasted by OVERRIDING instinct. Garbage IN means Garbage OUT NO MATTER how <u>SMART</u> we may BE. Being smart only makes us more cunning in defending our BIAS like DEBATERS, lobbyists, lawyers, and politicians, who try to be too smart for us to recognize their self-serving FALLACIES.

SO, we must CONSTANTLY be <u>UNFUSING EMOTION</u> from creatively intelligent symbolic scenarios and simulations of the real world, to FIND the most RELIABLE predictor of consequences to WORK for us individually and our society as a whole for TESTING by EXPERIMENT.

It is the PRIMARY role of personal religion in our FIREWALL to express instinctive emotion in ways that PROMOTE intelligent OBJECTIVITY so conscious intelligence can ACTUALIZE instinctive purpose, priority, and PASSION EFFECTIVELY.

CREATIVITY

HOWEVER, some PEOPLE are MORE INSTINCTIVELY EMOTIONAL or <u>EMOTIONALLY INTELLIGENT</u> or NUANCED than others or their UNCONSCIOUS INTELLIGENCE is more integrated with conscious intelligence and this MAY MAKE THEM more <u>CREATIVE</u> by the motivation, intensity, speed, diversity, discernment, differentiation, discrimination, multiplicity, and sophistication of their scenarioizing, simulating, and testing, so that they FIND more ultimately VALUABLE scenarios to be advanced to simulation and TESTING <u>FASTER</u> than LINEAR, logical, or rational, methods .

THEREFORE, the INSTINCTIVE EMOTIONS that MAKE us obsessive compulsive also DRIVE MOST scientific or social BREAKTHROUGHS or transcendent achievements of creative intelligence BECAUSE they accurately simulate OBJECTIVE REALITY in creatively intelligent ways. SO INSTINCTIVE CREATIVITY is a CORE VIRTUE in human nature that MUST be carefully PRESERVED and MANAGED through our personal religion, because it MUST NOT BE STOPPED, or we stop evolving and CREATING. Yet, it cannot be COMMANDED! It must be EVOLVED!

THIS MEANS we MUST have a VERY INTELLIGENT, aggregated COMMUNITY RELIGION and ORGANIZATION to integrate this COMPULSIVE DIVERSITY by recruiting GIFTED DIVERSE TALENT but KEEP these divergent potentials successfully organized, integrated, and WORKING TOGETHER for intelligently aggregated community GOALS the way our brain INTEGRATES our DIVERSE brain functions and neurons.

It is the role of PUBLIC RELIGION to INTEGRATE and organize DIVERSE lifestyles, values, instincts, emotions, personalities, abilities, talents, social relationships, functioning, etc., but the most CRITICAL PURPOSE is to create processes for DEMOCRATIC CREATION of OUR own PUBLIC RELIGIOUS THEOLOGY by CONSENSUS that decides community purpose, values, priorities, goals, methods, operations, etc.

46

COUNTER CONDITIONING

THE PRIMARY INSTINCTIVE EMOTION that fuses with SYMBOLS is FEAR because evolution works through DEATH, pain, and destruction, SO SURVIVAL reflexes DEMAND INSTANT REACTIONS BEFORE we have TIME to THINK creatively.

THEREFORE, FEAR is the INSTINCT that GOT CHEMICALLY EVOLVED and ELABORATED into SYMBOLIC INTELLIGENCE to give us PROACTIVE, preprogrammed, preemptive survival advantages and ultimately STIMULATES and DRIVES nearly ALL SYMBOLIC COGNITION even though IT mostly ACTS UNCONSCIOUSLY so our creative intelligence CAN make OBJECTIVE predictions not biased by the cellular chemistry of "fight or flight" and other "survival of the fittest" INSTINCTS.

THIS MEANS that the SYMBOLS that are BIASED by FEAR must be NEUTRALIZED by classical conditioning using rehearsal of religious beliefs in meditation, prayer, and ritual, or defensive intellectualized ANGER will ultimately EVOLVE into HATE disguised as SMART or LOVING but GETTING REVENGE.

THEREFORE, INTELLECTUALIZED ANGER must be carefully BALANCED by creative intelligence to JUST NEUTRALIZE the FEAR or ANGER will itself BIAS our OBJECTIVITY with HATE.

ALL similarly DISRUPTIVE EMOTIONS must also be COUNTER-CONDITIONED when CREATIVE INTELLIGENCE is NEEDED, including infatuation, envy, revenge, shame, sadism, ego, self-interest, ambition, etc. This also includes HOMEOSTATIC dysphoria like hunger, sleep loss, metabolic disorders, fatigue, or any sickness that impacts MOOD.

47

PROACTIVE CONDITIONING

PROACTIVE, PROSOCIAL SYMBOLS NEED to be POSITIVELY conditioned in childhood by LIFE EXPERIENCES that FACILITATE individual and aggregated creative INTELLIGENCE like valuing proven knowledge, broad education, full life experience, developmental maturity, reasoning, creativity, respecting and valuing other people's alternate points of view, accurate memory, scenarioizing, simulating, cause-effect-consequence links, science, empathy religious wisdom, ritual equality under law, etc., or it never GETS ACTIVATED or attached to MEMORY by conditioning SO it CAN be creatively RECALLED by the emotional component of metaphors, analogies, allusions, similarities, parables, images, and descriptions LATER IN LIFE when it is needed to understand or communicate to OTHER PEOPLE.

OTHERWISE PAIN may NOT TRIGGER adaptive FEAR, or FEAR may NOT give enough PRIORITY to danger or convert quickly enough to anger, or ANGER may NOT intelligently DEFEND us when we are ATTACKED, or SEXUAL ATTRACTION and response may NOT STRENGTHEN pair bonds and committed PARTNERSHIP, or LOVE may NOT INSPIRE PASSION for empathy, discipline, and resilience, or INFATUATION may NOT TRANSCEND self-centered ego, or instincts may NOT inspire WISE personal and public moral choices, or ENVY may NOT MOTIVATE disciplined ambition or cognitive dissonance may not intensify and discipline creative intelligence.

THEREFORE, FAMILY ACTIVITIES, RELATIONSHIPS, and DYNAMICS are CRITICALLY IMPORTANT for CHILDREN to condition symbolism that POSITIVELY contributes to the creative intelligence of their developing BELIEF SYSTEM, RELIGION, and individual FIREWALL that is INSTINCTIVE, INTUITIVE, EMPATHETIC, and OBJECTIVELY INTELLIGENT.

THIS IS PARTICULARLY IMPORTANT when a child's cellular chemistry is prone to PSYCHOPATHOLOGY or other diverse emotional chemistry that is ATYPICAL or absent like PSYCHOPATHS who must LEARN to simulate EMPATHY and COMPASSION while DECONDITIONING egotism and sadism. This includes people who have abusive SEXUAL compulsions, sadism, addictions, autism, are antisocial, bipolar, have borderline personality schizophrenia, or psychosis that do not respond to normal nurturing and guidance.

CONDITIONING and COUNTER-CONDITIONING by REHEARSAL is the way ACTORS learn to cry on cue and make us BELIEVE their performance. They use RECALLING memories of their own UNRELATED LIFE EXPERIENCE to produce body language that MAKES their CHARACTER and PLOT appear believable by COMPARTMENTALIZING their conscious awareness through disassociation.

THIS is how we NORMALLY FOCUS our attention and it means we can CHOOSE what to FOCUS ON, conditionally accept, believe, or suspend DIS-belief, in a narrow way EVEN IF IT IS NOT TRUE in the comprehensive context of our mind. We make decisions that DIVIDE our mind.

This is also how we STRATEGIZE religious theory to CONDITION EMOTIONS into intellectual symbols for a PASSIONATE commitment to a creatively intelligent BELIEF SYSTEM able to make objectively accurate predictions of the FUTURE and WORK we can do now to change it.

THE METHOD is to CONSCIOUSLY RECALL and REHEARSE EMOTION from unrelated experience while we consciously IMAGINE the interpretation, concept, or insight to be EMOTIONALLY conditioned or neutralized.

For example, I can't block the memory of my trauma from intruding my mind but I can BLOCK the emotional CRUSHING with EQUAL emotion from the memory of my INSIGHT into what was done to me. I FEEL the <u>WHOLE</u> TRUTH hidden then with pathological withdrawal but NEW understanding; let me FORGIVE THEM for being PSYCHOPATHS and ME for BELIEVING the SOUL CORRUPTING BLAME and PAIN they used to cover their abuse.

Knowing the TRUTH blew away the GUILT which had FROZEN my ABILITY to TRUST and FEEL anything but FEAR and HEALED me. Now I am FREE but CONVICTED to MAKE IT serve the MESSAGE of Jesus and ALL the SEEKERS of LOVE.

That releases the POWER of ALL TIME buried in my GENOME to survive and prosper living and partnering with others like me but DIFFERENT in ways I WILL RESPECT as I NURTURE them down a path that IS NOT MINE but which I LOVE for THEIR sake. When I am EMPTY I probably look like I am sulking, or brooding, but I kneel at the throne of TRUTH until my GENOME raises me up on a mission of LOVE from a LOVING GOD.

Conditioning can make us FEEL what we CHOOSE to believe.

The story can be IMAGINED for that specific situation but it MUST BE <u>TRUE</u> and guide the problematic instinctive emotions—<u>like a PARABLE</u>—into OBJECTIVELY intelligent resolution with appropriate emotions. This works using CLASSICAL CONDITIONING from meditation, daydreaming, prayer, etc.

However, strong INTENT to condition the HYPNOTIZED mind can CODE GENOME ACTIVATION in a SINGLE conditioning to rewire the brain.

48

DESTINY

Being smart enough to ACCURATELY predict the future does NOT take away our PERSONAL STRUGGLE to DECIDE on the BEST CHOICES for ACTION to control CONSEQUENCES. It just GIVES us the conditions, considerations, context, processes, priorities, motivations, purpose, goals, causes, science, consequences, resources, unique personality profile, and PREDICTIONS we MUST MAKE to intelligently strategize, integrate, and optimize our unique personality design and life experience to survive and prosper.

FREE WILL is a purely imaginary CYBERSPACE conception created in REBELLION against the rigid cause and effect RULE of this universe and our eventual destruction by mutation, entropy, and our own rigid cellular chemistry, so it ONLY exists in CYBERSPACE.

TRULY FREE WILL that stands outside the forces of physics and chemistry ONLY comes from the MUTATION of ENTROPY that created us winnowed by EVOLUTION. So ONLY A SPECIES can be free of the dead hand of this universe and WE must build an individual FIREWALL and FLY FREE in species CYBERSPACE before ENTROPY gets us.

WE are EACH CHEMICAL COMPUTERS and we MUST GIVE UP the idea that we can significantly CHANGE our neuron circuit functioning as EASILY as we change brand names JUST BY

CONSCIOUS CHOICE or INSIGHT because computer programs are COMPLETELY separate from the machine that runs it and similarly our intellect has LITTLE control over our chemical program of instinctive emotions that DRIVE our survival and prosperity. SO, we CANNOT JUDGE EVERYONE by one standard of sincere or genuine effort to change or adapt. BLAME is the tool of psychopaths to serve their greed or revenge, not TEACHERS or MANAGERS.

SO, it is HOPELESS, pointless, and foolish to BLAME people for doing what they are PROGRAMMED to do as chemical computers. Chemical programming is RIGID, and sincere, genuine, intelligent effort CAN MAKE LITTLE DIFFERENCE. Failure and dysfunction in the community should just be PRAGMATICALLY reprogrammed with operant conditioning, new jobs, restructured privileges, and obligations, or given psychopathic placement.

The AGGREGATED INTELLIGENCE of our species was designed by EVOLUTION to work depending on DIVERSITY of FUNDAMENTAL mental processes INTELLIGENTLY INTEGRATED in the larger community to provide the FLEXIBILITY to QUICKLY adapt our community organization to purely SYMBOLIC insights or concepts BECAUSE it is VERY difficult for our conscious mind to INFLUENCE our chemical HARDWARE. We must often RECRUIT NEW LEADERS with CHEMISTRY and LIFE EXPERIENCE COMPATIBLE with CRITICAL JOBS or new strategies because they CANNOT be TRAINED or EARN the special mental abilities.

The PRAGMATIC success of EXPERIMENTALLY VERIFIED PROBLEM SOLVING must pick our LEADERS or OBJECTIVITY will be CORRUPTED by the DEAD HAND of SENIORITY, chain of command, politics, tradition, culture, past rationalizations, THEORY, or ACADEMIC SUPERHEROES.

Otherwise psychopaths will MANIPULATE their way into control using CROWD EMOTIONS like EMPATHY, IDENTITY FUSION, or other INSTINCTS to BLOCK OBJECTIVITY and ENTROPY WILL RULE.

The OBJECTIVE WISDOM of <u>EVOLUTION</u> must continue to be the measure for future SURVIVAL and PROSPERITY because ENTROPY ULTIMATELY RULES our universe and we still have FAR to go before species level intelligence becomes self-aware but it is clear that TECHNOLOGY, FREE COMMUNICATION, MASSIVE SIMULATION, and SUPER COMPUTERS are going to NETWORK our species with EXTREME creative intelligence which requires MEANING, PURPOSE, and PRIORITY, which CAN <u>ONLY</u> come from our ANCIENT GENOME EXPRESSED as EMOTION through our SELF-CONDITIONING with RELIGION.

49

FIREWALL

However, to be effectively <u>CREATIVE</u>, conscious intelligence MUST FUNCTION independently of INSTINCT because our emotions are chemically DEFINITIVE and CORRUPT the HYPOTHETICAL symbolic process of FAST scenarioizing, simulating, and evaluating the MASSIVE NUMBER of predictions that creative intelligence must make to FIND ones that are LIKELY to OBJECTIVELY serve our needs SO that our LIMITED ABILITY to CORROBORATE and TEST possibilities is NOT OVERWHELMED.

EVOLUTION ORIGINALLY DESIGNED our HOMEOSTATIC biological regulation to AUTOMATICALLY REGULATE health issues that need constant adjustment in a predictable way like body temperature, breathing, heart rate, hunger, sleep, digestion, metabolism, and PROCESSING of vision, touch, movement, space, smell, hearing, emotions, and instincts, UNCONSCIOUSLY, so our conscious mind is NOT DISTRACTED or DISRUPTED by the REGULATION of our body or sensory experiences.

THEREFORE, there is already a DEFACTO WALL between the purely symbolic simulations of intelligence and the physical cellular chemistry of instinctive emotion, much like the difference between computer hardware and operating program.

SO, our INTELLIGENCE can turn this into a FIREWALL between EMOTION and INTELLECT that PREVENTS our instinctive subconscious IMPERATIVES from CRIPPLING our OBJECTIVE intelligence with instinctive EMOTION AND helps objective intelligence to nurture our subconscious with reason so it can recognize and give pragmatic PASSION to INTELLECT to OUTSMART all the threats to survival and prosperity.

This is the PURPOSE religion EVOLVED to serve but psychopaths co-opted and CORRUPTED it to serve their own PERSONAL greed for power and sadism over other people.

INSTINCT is NOT OBJECTIVE ENOUGH to KNOW HOW to POLICE this FIREWALL SO it is up to our OBJECTIVE INTELLIGENCE to learn to discern, differentiate, and discriminate between what EMOTIONAL EXPERIENCE of instinct is HELPFUL in initiating and guiding PURPOSE for symbolic intelligence to ACHIEVE or WHAT is better KEPT HIDDEN in our sub-conscious mind BEHIND our personal FIREWALL using religion to prevent DISRUPTION of the conscious OBJECTIVE symbolic processes of creative intelligence.

DESIGNING, strengthening, and disciplining this FIREWALL is the goal of MATURATION, family emotional conditioning, religion, self-discipline, self-improvement, personal growth, PSYCHOLOGICAL CONSULTATION, therapy, and psychological intervention.

THE GENERAL CHANGE RULE is that what is LEARNED from life experience CAN be changed by life experience but what is CAUSED by or results in chemistry MUST USUALLY be CHANGED by chemistry.

Evolution designed the FIREWALL to MEDIATE between emotion and thinking. Much of that is done in sleep and dreaming. However, it SHOULD be followed by careful symbolic analysis, evaluation, and INTERVENTION if needed using De- or Re-conditioning, meditation, daydreaming or PRAYER to neutralize EMOTIONAL CORRUPTION of creative intelligence.

Yet, we have LITTLE CONTROL over instinct or emotion and it is mostly up to our conscious intelligence to accommodate and adapt behavior to SERVE instinct.

THEREFORE, the STRATEGY of building a creatively intelligent FIREWALL must be to STRENGTHEN what cellular CHEMISTRY already USES for homeostatic regulation that ALLOWS subconscious processes to DO simple, preprogrammed, reflexive problem solving, like HABIT that does NOT disrupt the creative symbolic PROCESSES of our CONSCIOUS intellect.

We make habits that GUIDE our intellect to CREATE a symbolic CONTEXT for survival and prosperity our SUBCONSCIOUS mind can agree with and CONDITION with congruent emotions using religion to MOTIVATE the resilient obsession, objectivity, and self-discipline of CREATIVE INTELLIGENCE.

HOWEVER, THERE MUST be an EFFICIENT PARTNERSHIP between CONSCIOUS and UNCONSCIOUS functions that EMPOWERS BOTH to SERVE their evolutionary design.

LOVING OUR WORK

This happens easily and automatically if we <u>LOVE</u> WHAT we ARE DOING or THINKING because it is always on our mind as we take care of business and run simulations or do thought experiments looking for planning or management options. We are in a TIMELESS SPACE where we are NOT EVEN CONSCIOUS of the hours, days, months, or years. It is a refuge we SEEK at every opportunity our stressful lives give and it REFRESHES us with the oxytocin, endorphin, dopamine, vasopressin of CREATING, so EUPHORIA follows insight and REWARDS the STRUGGLE, whether we VALIDATE a theory, achieve a goal, paint a picture, make a baby, or NOT.

LOVE makes PLEASURE of it ALL.

WHEN INTELLECT FOLLOWS EMOTION

However, the PREOCCUPATION of DAYDREAMING can become DESTRUCTIVE if we let our conscious mind seek out and PASSIVELY follow a DYSPHORIC MOOD generated by BOREDOM, pain, and homeostatic or UNCONSCIOUS conflict we allow to STAY unconscious.

MEDITATION, DAYDREAMING, and PRAYER WORK to change emotions BECAUSE our CONSCIOUS creative intelligence RUNS on classically conditioned SYMBOLS, NOT SENSORY EXPERIENCE, or the real world our senses report. Senses just PROVIDE the electricity and metabolism for the epigenetic memory chemistry for our SOUL to FLY into symbolic CYBERSPACE.

SLEEP and DREAMING are the default EVOLUTIONARY FIREWALL for MEDIATING memory, emotions, instinct, interpretation, and intellect, BUT it NEEDS to be CONTINUED in the waking state to COPE with our highly SYMBOLIZED, INTELLIGENCE ENHANCED, SOCIALLY COMPLEX, HIGH CHALLENGE TECHNICAL LIVES.

It comes AUTOMATICALLY with INTRUSIVE memories and disruptive emotions so we MUST CHOOSE to OBJECTIVELY investigate, INTERPRET, and conclude when INTRUSIVE memories, feelings, or thoughts are a WARNING or an OPPORTUNITY.

HOW INTELLIGENCE WORKS

IF INTELLIGENT ANALYSIS of CONFLICT between intellect and emotion yields NO PLAN of resolution or action FAILS to RESOLVE dysphoria or pain, our mind AMPLIFIES the dysphoria and EXPANDS associated memory recall for analysis with CREATIVE generation of RESOLUTION hypothesis and scenarios for SIMULATION till one predicts reduction and can be TRANSLATED into a TEST for an action PLAN.

IF the DYSPHORIA is STILL NOT RESOLVED, the AMPLIFICATION CONTINUES to BUILD INTENSITY with classical conditioning (brooding) until the ANXIETY of cognitive dissonance FORCES our intellect to evaluate the homeostatic PRIORITY and either FORCES IT to become UNCONSCIOUS through repression and denial OR, if the dysphoria is TRAUMA INDUCED, IT AUTOMATICALLY locks on a FULLY CONSCIOUS OBSESSION and a COMPULSION to ACT because SURVIVAL instincts OVERRIDE homeostatic regulation.

THE WAY OUT of this TRAP is to USE SENSORY MEMORIES, religious conditioning, and STORY simulation as <u>SYMBOLS</u> that SIMULATE a CREATIVELY intelligent resolution USING rehearsal, repetition, habit formation, MEDITATION, DAYDREAMING, or PRAYER with symbolized, SIMULATED, safe exposure to the trauma that KEEPS our conscious INTELLECT in CONTROL by using religious conditioning in a SIMULATED STORY resolution until our brain BUILDS new neurons, axons, synapses, and neurological circuits ABLE to IMITATE the symbolic resolution unconsciously with NEW NEURONAL CIRCUITS.

53

DIVERSITY

EACH of these COMPLEX and DIVERSE cellular processes FALL along a distribution of DEGREE so EVERYONE has a UNIQUE combination of instinctive processes and intensity that COMBINE to constitute their <u>PROFILE</u> of gnomically defined PERSONALITY with specific VARIETIES in abstract, social, and emotional intelligence, obsessiveness, compulsiveness, creativity, inspiration, social instincts, belief systems, energy level, schizophrenia, autism, and every other form of symbolic processing and EMOTIONAL RESPONSE found in the CYBERSPACE and CELLULAR CHEMISTRY of our species.

TRAUMA, ABUSE, and PSYCHOLOGICAL SHOCK also CHANGES the behavioral EXPRESSION of cellular chemistry because it CHANGES the functioning and development of the brain and NEUROLOGICAL CIRCUITS at all ages.

THE resulting VARIATION in behavioral PERSONALITY gives EVERYONE unique functioning INCLUDING psychopaths and those who are bipolar. Emotional diversity from our sexually recombinant genome, life experience, and mutation GUARANTEES "just the right" combination for ALL emotional and intellectual needs of our community, BUSINESS, and GOVERNMENT somewhere in our species.

We need STRONGLY EMPATHIC people who can negotiate social discord and conflict. We need leaders, and scientists, and all the workers that keep our world safe and prosperous. IN FACT, WE NEED EVERYONE! We need them to INCREASE the diversity NECESSARY to maintain the MASSIVE populations, TECHNOLOGY, SCIENCE, and LEADERSHIP, REQUIRED to survive and prosper when our MASSIVE POPULATION needs more than we got.

DEVIATIONS from social NORMS have been PRESERVED in our species reproductive pool and culture BECAUSE they can be CRITICALLY valuable in COMBINATION with typically functional abilities to MAKE technological breakthroughs, organizational adaptations, and social insights during unpredictable species CRISES such as environmental disasters, economic collapse, social revolution, technological innovation, disease, or war, even when they ARE DESTRUCTIVE in every normal context.

54

RECRUITMENT

ALL our CULTURE has to DO is RECRUIT people with the right combination of cellular chemistry, life experience, and achievements from our great diversity of people to CREATE an instant MIRACLE LEADER or conceptual breakthrough for our species that CANNOT be produced by ANY creative intelligence, EDUCATION, SCIENCE, value system, belief, religion, civilization, tradition, theory, strategy, research, proactive culture organization artificially intelligent computer or PERSONAL WEALTH.

Only the OBJECTIVITY of ENTROPY can produce the FULL range of CREATIVITY for EVOLUTION to WINNOW for survival and prosperity so our SPECIES can continue to its DESTINY by recruiting genius and leadership.

TO MAINTAIN this DIVERSE POOL we must MAKE ROOM for EVERY KIND of HUMAN willing to TRY to CONTRIBUTE to society by WORKING for the COMMON GOOD.

BRILLIANT RECRUITMENT DEMONSTRATES EVIDENCE of how organized AGGREGATED SPECIES level INTELLIGENCE can be FAR SUPERIOR in ADVANCING community and species SURVIVAL and PROSPERITY with democratic processes BUT the BENEFICIAL result of RECRUITMENT may be MISINTERPRETED and INFATUATED into dysfunctional HERO WORSHIP to be supernatural, genius, brilliance, inspiration, MESSIAH, or willpower, when it was ACTUALLY SPECIFIC cellular chemistry or UNIQUE life experience inevitable in our diverse species and DELIBERATELY NURTURED and RECRUITED by CREATIVELY INTELLIGENT social organization which SEARCHED for and FOUND the ALREADY DEVELOPED cellular chemistry and life experience for critical jobs from the DIVERSE pool of our species.

OUR PRAISE and GRATITUDE should GO to the RECRUITMENT PROCESS NOT the CIRCUMSTANCE of the best combination of ABILITIES because that is often CAUSED by the entropy and mutation of UNIQUE or DEVIANT family, life experience, or cellular chemistry functions and SHOULD NOT or CANNOT BE EMULATED in the society as a whole BECAUSE our aggregated SOCIETY MUST REMAIN DIVERSE to satisfy the requirements of feeding and housing seven billion DIFFERENT people DEEPLY BELIEVING DIFFERENTLY with COMPUTER ASSISTED survival and prosperity.

The brilliance of PRODIGY, genius, or MESSIAH is not a CHOICE, SELF DISCIPLINE, or SACRIFICE to be CELEBRATED as an IDEAL but is an INEVITABLE evolution of PERSONAL DESTINY in the NURTURING CONTEXT of DIVERSE species intelligence LIVING by LOVE.

RECRUITMENT is the METHOD cattle, sheep, goat, pig, crop, and chicken ranchers, or SLAVERS have DONE for thousands of years to survive and EXPAND their prosperity WITHOUT the NEED to recruit educated or nurtured GENIUS, technical innovation, personal wealth, or INTERVENTION by a SUPERNATURAL GOD. THEY JUST TOOK the best, and let evolution take the rest.

WARLORDS and OVERLORDS just searched for and ENSLAVED or BOUGHT SAVANTS, GENIUSES, or gifted people, like LEONARDO DE VINCI or MICHAEL ANGELO, and BILLIONAIRES still do it to OUTWIT exploited workers and CLAIM the CREDIT as EVIDENCE of THEIR OWN SUPERIORITY just like the Medici's did. They AWED EVERYONE with GOD'S TRUTH in the BRILLIANT ART.

PSYCHOPATHS ESPECIALLY love hiring consultants and holding money over their heads to see how high and far they can get them to JUMP to get what they FEEL LIKE turned into JUSTIFICATION. MONEY is VOTES, and it CAN CORRUPT creative intelligence when we have no personal religion.

FINDING WISDOM

HOWEVER, INSTINCTIVE PERSONALITY can CHANGE within UNPREDICTABLE limits BECAUSE it ARISES out of cellular chemistry that also controls LIFELONG GENESIS of our brain growing new neurons, axons, and synapsis that establish new "neuronal circuits" EVERY TIME we have new life experiences and LEARN new behaviors or beliefs while old connections that are no longer USED are trimmed or DESTROYED.

OUR GOAL must be to INTEGRATE a COMPLETE SELF-AWARENESS in the FIREWALL of our fully conscious IDENTITY with BOTH emotion AND OBJECTIVE intelligence which MEANS our symbolic INTELLECT must take LEADERSHIP to INTERPRET objective TRUTH to create religious theory compatible with our SUBCONSCIOUS instincts using learning, science, religious theory, mediation, meditation, daydreaming, and prayer.

RELIGION and SCIENCE are the SAME in the sense that they are both ARTIFICIAL and ARBITRARY SYMBOLIC simulations, theories, or analogs of ideas or concepts that TAKE their MEANING and SIGNIFICANCE from ACCURATELY PREDICTING a future that GIVES us choices NOW to WORK for a more satisfying and FULFILLING LIFE both as an individual and species.

MESSIAH

THERE is a GREATER CHARACTER TYPE in the diverse cellular chemistry of human nature that UNITES intelligence, empathy, creativity, infatuation, charisma, courage, and charm to MAKE a TRULY GREAT human VISIONARY able to LEAD our SPECIES to become the TRANSCENDENT SELF-AWARENESS our highest dreams are made of and religions have always been BUILT on.

THIS KIND of PERSON has been CONCEIVED OVER and OVER in folk WISDOM of every culture around camp fires and in communal houses to be a <u>MESSIAH</u> that FULFILLS the HERO WORSHIP we know as children or hopeless victims and many people have TRIED to BECOME that person and some like JESUS, MOHAMED, BUDDHA, CONFUCIUS, KRISHNA, GANDHI, and many others MAY have achieved it.

This is BECAUSE personality ARISES out of CELLULAR CHEMISTRY which is an EVOLUTIONARY process influenced by the LIFELONG GENESIS of new neurons MAKING, trimming, and ORGANIZING new axons and synapsis from STEM cells that MAKE NEW neurological circuits PATTERNED epigenetically by our BEHAVIOR and SYMBOLIC BELIEFS in CYBERSPACE.

OUR PURELY SYMBOLIC BELIEFS, SELF-DISCIPLINE, and WORK CAN POTENTIALLY MAKE ANY of us TRANSCENDENT no matter WHAT ELSE has gone on in our skull from our childhood, life experience, education, resources, health, cellular chemistry, community, culture, and government that may have limited or CORRUPTED our mental, social, or real-world SUCCESS.

WE may NOT BECOME a MESSIAH but we MIGHT RECOGNIZE, FOLLOW, BELIEVE and make TRANSCENDENT LOVE REAL in CYBERSPACE.

57

GOVERNMENT

THE CREATIVELY INTELLIGENT ORGANIZATIONAL PROCESSES of our SPECIES must be FACILITATED by FORMAL OBLIGATORY social organization and supportive CULTURAL values that CAPITALIZE on the inherent HUMAN DIVERSITY to RECRUIT the best person for every job in our evolving, technologically complex community ORGANIZATION of government, business, social culture, and species intelligence.

IN THE PAST, war, murder, trauma, coercion, extortion, and intimidation DID this FACILITATION but VICTIMIZING DISRUPTS the personal INVESTMENT and vital TRUST in our community governance that we must have to justify our support and sacrifice in a self-run DEMOCRATIC government.

However, now our WORK FORCE is BILLIONS of people going from job to job who sometimes live in poverty FEELING like TRASH mixed with BLOOD while the rich live in a WORLD exactly of their choosing CLAIMING they DESERVE to have anything they want for BUYING the smart REAL ESTATE or INSURANCE consultants and financial advisors with OTHER people's money and the LAW can't touch them. They were either born into it or their children are, and they are SELF RIGHTEOUS ABOUT IT.

ORGANIZATION and FACILITATION of INDIVIDUAL INTELLIGENCE into an aggregated intelligent network for governance must be DONE by our primary social ORGANIZATIONS MEDIATING a governing FIREWALL of relationships between different work and social activities by EXAMINING documented HISTORY and repeatable EXPERIMENTS to EVALUATE the cause and effect of the SAME KIND of organizational PROCEDURES that CREATED our high technology using COMPETITIVELY superior WORK organizations.

THIS is the SAME WAY our brain integrates DIFFERENT types of neurons to PERFORM different homeostatic SUBCONSCIOUS processes that COMBINE to CREATE our intelligent, SELF-AWARE IDENTITY as an INDIVIDUAL with a SOUL.

THE SEPARATION of TEACHERS from LEARNERS, bosses from workers, overlords from slaves, and predators from prey is inherent to EVOLUTION creating and WINNOWING the DIVERSITY for our species to SURVIVE great long-term CHANGE.

THEREFORE, the EVOLUTION of creatively intelligent social AUTHORITY and our SUBMISSION to it HAD to be DICTATED by our CELLULAR CHEMISTRY or our dependable COMPLIANCE to AGGREGATED social intelligence would simply BE OVERTHROWN by EVERY individually self-aware and creatively intelligent person JUST LIKE PSYCHOPATHS ALREADY DO.

This community intelligence must have AUTHORITY from a RELIGIOUS CONSENSUS following democratic evolutionary derived THEORY that structures COMMUNITY LIFE.

GOVERNMENT LAWS MUST BE CREATED, MODIFIED, and UPDATED by a DEMOCRATIC evolutionary PROCESS of members VOTING to constitute LAW MAKERS GUARDED by PUBLIC RELIGION and have its own FIREWALL like a CONSTITUTION to

PREVENT UNCONSCIOUS "crowd" emotions like empathy, fear, or anger, from aggregating under PSYCHOPATHS and PERVERTING the democratic process to OVERRIDE objective species intelligence with PSYCHOPATHOLOGY that will start the next WAR with HATE or GREED.

58

DICTATORS

AUTHORITARIAN GOVERNMENTS run by strongmen, dictators, warlords, oligarchs, revolutionaries, and hidden conspirators are the TURF of PSYCHOPATHS and they MAKE IT their business to DESTROY the POSSIBILITY of higher level, emotional, or creative intelligence in every competitor.

PSYCHOPATHS GUARDING EGREGIOUS WEALTH and social POWER extoll self-discipline, will power, hard work, heroism, self-sacrifice, courage, creativity, intelligence, or religion as the SOURCE of their WEALTH.

HOWEVER, THESE are EXCUSES, RATIONALIZATIONS, DECEPTIONS, and ALIBIES NO ONE can DISPROVE for why NO ONE ELSE should BENEFIT from their CIRCUMSTANCE and OPPORTUNISTIC RUTHLESSNESS in PREEMPTING and DIVERTING the enormous resources of EVERYBODY'S JOB, INCOME, lifestyle, community, beliefs, freedom, history, culture, civilization, and species intelligence.

THEIR CREATIVE INSIGHT and RESULTING RESOURCES BELONG in the FULL SOCIAL CONTEXT and COMPLETE economic DYNAMICS that PRODUCED it JUST LIKE EVERYONE ELSE'S <u>WORK</u> does to EMPATHICALLY and COMPASSIONATELY

RUN our culture, technology, civilization, GOVERNMENT, and SPECIES INTELLIGENCE for the GENERATIONS to come.

PSYCHOPATHS BREAK DOWN the social STRUCTURE of DEMOCRATIC PROCESSES and INSTALL some form of AUTHORITARIANISM which INEVITABLY becomes dysfunctional and is OVERTHROWN because they have LITTLE or NO motivation or EMPATHIC understanding of the INSTINCTS that DRIVE the network of communications, social relationships, and processes of AGGREGATED, SOCIALLY ORGANIZED INTELLIGENCE.

59

AYN RAND

THE WRITER AYN RAND is an EXAMPLE of PSYCHOPATHIC GOVERNMENT THEORY.

MONEY, POWER, and EGOTISM is HER GOD and RICH people WORSHIP her justification of SELFISHNESS and GREED as the GREATEST human VIRTUE and achievement. She even claims POOR people BENEFIT from BEING enslaved, exploited, and VICTIMIZED, because it kept them from starving to death.

SHE THINKS COMMUNITIES are STUPID and SHOULD be BROKEN UP into isolated individuals who COMPETE and FIGHT each other instead of cooperating and she thinks it is JUSTIFIED to STARVE the poor and DENY them resources to FORCE them to SUBMIT to EXPLOITATION in FEAR of privation, or LUST for reward, BECAUSE she thinks their circumstantial, financial, psychological POVERTY and HELPLESSNESS is <u>DESERVED</u>.

RAND'S HEROES ARE robber barons, psychopaths, and warlords designed by evolution to DOMINATE anywhere; RUTHLESSNESS and "fight to the DEATH" is the greatest VIRTUE because they get to KILL YOU and take ALL your stuff.

THE LIBERTARIAN societies that RAND would ESTABLISH inevitably EVOLVES a SINGLE WARLORD or conspiracy government that COMMANDEERS control of resources and power to ENSLAVE everyone else with FEAR, BRIBERY, and DECEPTION, but makes them EXPENDABLE at their CONVENIENCE.

THE ONLY TIME RICH or SELF-MADE people NURTURE the needs of POOR people is when they ARE so RICH or POWERFUL that MONEY or ITS POWER needs POLITICAL INFLUENCE to OPERATE or ceases to be EMOTIONALLY SATISFYING ENOUGH and they decide to COMPETE for EMOTIONAL social AGGRANDIZEMENT like our current president, or ACT OUT HATE in the social or POLITICAL arena by manipulating social EMPATHY and INSTINCTIVE EMOTION like FEAR or GREED.

RAND INSISTS that those who GET GREAT POWER will ENCOURAGE others to GET similar POWER but the PROCESS that allows people to get RICH and POWERFUL favors COMPETITION and the VIRTUE of CONFLICT that LEAVES POOR people HELPLESS against great wealth, resources, consultants, DEMOGRAPHICS, SUPER COMPUTERS, and GUNS.

THE RICH only want WORKERS with NO ABILITY or RIGHT to OPPOSE their own SELF-AGGRANDIZEMENT or follow a DIFFERENT personal or social CONCEPT. RICH PEOPLE even CLAIM GOD or other AUTHORITY-CENTERED belief systems like FASCISM that JUSTIFY the POLITICS of personality, power, militarism, control, fear, revenge, and manipulation.

THEY TAKE OVER the GOD BUSINESS in every CHURCH and LEADERSHIP in every government using any SELF-RIGHTEOUS rationalization, their VICTIMS are dumb enough to BELIEVE.

THEY BUY CHURCHES and POLITICAL CAMPAIGNS to TEACH our children to GO to CHURCH and OBEY their AUTHORITARIAN IDEA of social organization, GOVERNMENT, and PATRIOTIC COMPLIANCE, like GOD-FEARING SHEEP

USING rationalizations, justifications, manipulation, deception, lies, and FEAR.

THEY FIRST TAKE OVER the GOVERNMENT by OPPOSING IT JUST LIKE the COMMUNISTS DID in Russia, China, and Cambodia, or the Nazis DID in PRE-WAR GERMANY AND the RICH RIGHT WING "CONSERVATIVES" have done NOW in OUR COUNTRY.

LIVE LONG AND PROSPER!

www.ingramcontent.com/pod-product-compliance
Lightning Source LLC
Chambersburg PA
CBHW061655120626
46550CB00003B/946